Decisions, Decisions…

A Handbook for Judicial Writing

DECISIONS, DECISIONS...

A HANDBOOK FOR JUDICIAL WRITING

LOUISE MAILHOT
JUSTICE OF THE QUÉBEC COURT OF APPEAL

AND

JAMES D. CARNWATH
REGIONAL SENIOR JUDGE, ONTARIO COURT OF JUSTICE (GENERAL DIVISION)

PREFACE BY DR. JAMES C. RAYMOND
THE UNIVERSITY OF ALABAMA

LES ÉDITIONS YVON BLAIS INC.

C.P. 180 Cowansville (Québec) Canada
Tél.: (450) 266-1086 FAX: (450) 263-9256

Canadian Cataloguing in Publication Data

Mailhot, Louise, 1940-

Decisions, decisions –: a handbook for judicial writing

Translation of: Écrire la décision.

Includes bibliographical references and index.

ISBN 2-89451-237-6

1. Legal composition. 2. Judgments – Language. 3. Law – Quebec (Province) – Language. 4. Law – Language. I. Carnwath, James D. II. Title.

K94.M3413 1998 808'06634 C98-940326-2

Legal Deposit: 1st trimester 1998
National Library of Canada
Bibliothèque nationale du Québec

ISBN: 2-89451-237-6

To all those charged with listening patiently, deciding fairly, and explaining persuasively, we dedicate this handbook.

CONTENTS

PREFACE

It was a Frenchman who spoiled us: Michel Eyquem de Montaigne. Montaigne is traditionally credited with the invention of a new form of writing, the essay, a genre that allows us to imagine real human beings on both sides of the text. On the writer's side, an ordinary individual – not a theologian or a magistrate or a scholar – but a neighbor, a friendly amateur with a personal take on the subject at hand, motivated by an urge to communicate, not to intimidate or to impress. On the readers' side, ordinary people, friends and neighbors who do not particularly need the information or the writer's take on it, but who welcome it the way they would welcome a letter from a person with interesting opinions. All essays provide an illusion of intimacy; an illusion because we usually have no personal acquaintance with the authors, and yet they address us as if we did. This fictional intimacy, more than the form of the essay, is perhaps the most remarkable aspect of Montaigne's invention.

Nowadays we take the public intimacy of essays for granted. We encounter it daily on editorial pages and in signed articles in our better newspapers and magazines. We know that good writers can write about any subject with clarity and grace, that they can explain even the mysteries of black holes and double helixes in language that any educated non-scientist can understand, at least to the degree that these things can be understood at all. In fact, we have come to expect this sort of intimacy in writing. We may forgive scientists and engineers and technicians for their jargon as long as they confine it to books and journals intended for other specialists. But we will not tolerate it in writing they expect us, non-specialists, to read and understand. We want them to address us in plain English. We know it can be done because good journalists and talented scientists have demonstrated time and again the power of ordinary language to make technical matters comprehensible to ordinary readers.

We who are outside the legal profession, amateurs like myself, feel the same way about legal writing. We who are expected to obey what we read are properly offended when lawyers compose contracts or statutes or orders or decrees or judgments in archaic and sometimes foreign phrases. We know it does not have to be that way, because we have seen it done otherwise. We have read accurate and interesting accounts of legal matters in ordinary newspapers and magazines. We have read Holmes and Denning and Dickson, all of whom have welcomed us into the logic of the law, making it seem like a set of common-sense principles in plain language designed to help ordinary citizens lead orderly, peaceful, and secure lives.

Attorneys and judges have been known to defend the peculiar language of the law on the ground that it has been refined and made precise by centuries of usage. But we outsiders are not persuaded. We suspect that lawyers use the old language at times because it is conveniently available in form books, or because it makes them sound like lawyers, or because they are blissfully unaware of how odd it really is, or because they think it will fill us outsiders with awe and a willingness to pay handsomely for documents beyond our ken. We even suspect that on occasion lawyers themselves do not understand the language of the law; not one lawyer in ten knows the difference between a "will" and a "testament", for example, but they will cling to both words like voodoo votaries casting a spell, afraid that a single omission will spoil the charm and render it ineffective for reasons they do not fully understand.

Wherever I lecture on legal writing, I try to find a local author to propose as a model: "Why Can't Lawyers Write Like X", I tell my audience, inserting the name of an author the audience is likely to admire. In New Zealand, I used Katherine Mansfield as a model. In Halifax, Hugh MacLennan. Of course there are many valid answers to this question, including the obvious ones that lawyers are not writing for entertainment, that they are not writing fiction, that their dockets are overwhelming, and so on. But I ask the question anyway, on the theory that some qualities are shared by *all* good writing, regardless of genre. The first-century rhetorician Marcus Fabius Quintilian once said as much: "all eloquence has something in common; and that shared quality is what we should imitate."[1]

This book is an extension of that classic pedagogy. When Justices Mailhot and Carnwath advise their colleagues on the bench to "Write in a simple and coherent language", to "Avoid old-fashioned expressions", to "Use the active voice", to "Use a variety of short and long sentences and paragraphs" (we could add the entire table of contents), they are merely describing the practice of all good writers. But they also provide specifics in the context of the law. Anyone could say, "Write like Margaret Atwood" – but, let's face it, if judges could write like Margaret Atwood just by choosing to do so, no doubt they would. Judges need examples. They need advice about those details that distinguish good writing from tiresome drivel, nuances of craft that generally escape our attention when we read because good writers generally take pains to conceal their artifice, to make their art seem easier than it really is. This is the sort of advice you will find in the chapters that follow.

Almost all the rules in this book could be summarized in what might be called two great commandments: write like a person (not like a judge or an attorney); and think of your reader as an ordinary friend or neighbor (not a collective or an abstraction like "Plaintiff" or "Court of Appeal", or "Readers of Law Reports", or "The Press"). Obviously you will need to use legal terminology when there is no handy equivalent in ordinary English. But when there is an equivalent, use it – just as you would if you were discussing the matter with a friend or family member untrained in Law. This is the way Montaigne imagined himself and his readers. He *inhabits* his style. We know him as an individual: "I am the subject of this book" ("*ie suis moy-mesme la matière de mon livre*") he tells us in his preface to the first edition. And his readers are "family and friends" ("parens & amis")[2] – an obvious fiction, since if he really had been writing for friends and family, he would hardly

1. Of course he said it in Latin, which in the spirit of this book we will relegate to a footnote: "*Habet tamen omnis eloquentia aliquid commune; it imitemur quod commune est.*" *The Tenth and Twelfth Books of the Institutions of Quintilian*. Ed. Henry S. Frieze. New York: American, 1911. X, 2,22 (p. 59).
2. *Essais* (Bordeaux: Millange, 1580), preface.

have gone to the trouble of having his essays printed and sold. But it is a useful fiction, one that allowed him to write for perfect strangers *as if* they were friends and family. Therein lies the secret of his style.

Centuries later Hugh MacLennan echoed Montaigne's approach to writing when he reflected on his own. The essay, he tells us, is a genre that

> depends more than any other form of writing on a relationship between author and reader so close that at times the author at his desk has the illusion that he is lounging in his library late in the evening of a well-spent day, a glass of beer at his elbow and a personal friend in the opposite chair.[3]

If judges could adopt this pose in their writing, they would need little other advice. But the pose is just that, a posture, an assumed persona that requires a bit of acting. And not everyone has a knack for playing the role of themselves when they write. Once we start putting words on a page or computer screen, we are tempted to become someone else, someone a bit more formal, a bit more learned, perhaps a bit stuffier than the persons we are around the house and on the golf course and at the grocery store. It is very hard to divest ourselves of the professional pose when we are writing about professional matters. But this is, in fact, what the best essayists have always done, and the best jurists as well, the judges whose work we like to read, whose work has made a difference in the legal profession precisely because it is both intelligible and memorable.

This is a book for judges who are not afraid to write like human beings, for judges who have enough confidence in their knowledge of the law to express it on paper in the same plain language they would use in talking with a neighbor who happens to ask a legal question across the fence on a Saturday afternoon. Not all judges have this degree of confidence; this book is for those who do. And although it is addressed primarily to judges, its

3. "Prologue: The Writer and His Audience." In *The Other Side of Hugh MacLennan: Selected Essays Old and New*. Ed. Elspeth Cameron. Toronto: Macmillan of Canada, 1978, p. 3.

precepts apply to everyone who writes in or about the law. "Decisions, Decisions" – well yes, of course, but also contracts, grants, quitclaims, statutes, motions, letters, indictments, mortgages, wills, traffic tickets – all the legal documents that non-lawyers have to read and understand.

I cannot pretend to be an objective reader of this book, since I consider myself its metaphorical grandfather. Both Justice Mailhot and Justice Carnwath were, while not exactly students of mine, certainly present when I have lectured to legal writing classes over many years. When I find passages that resemble something I may have said in those lectures, I feel the sort of proprietary satisfaction we all feel when we recognize ourselves in progeny who are entirely themselves, but who reveal a kinship in some small way, even if it is only in the shape of an eyebrow or a peculiar note in their laughter. This is a wholly original book, of course, but it is also emblematic of a long friendship and collaboration among the three of us who have worked together in one capacity or another in judgement writing seminars for new and experienced federally appointed judges in Canada since 1982. Here's hoping that it will serve as a pleasant and useful reminder of those seminars for the numerous friends we have made in the course of teaching them, and a pleasant and useful introduction to those we hope to meet in years to come.

James C. Raymond
Professor
The University of Alabama

ACKNOWLEDGEMENTS

In July of 1981, the Canadian Institute for the Administration of Justice organized the first judgment writing seminar in Canada. The authors were among the fortunate judges in attendance. The initial enthusiasm for the seminar continues to the present, under the auspices of the C.I.A.J.

There swiftly followed a course for Francophones, conceived and established by Madam Justice Mailhot. In 1984, Mr. Justice Carnwath assumed responsibility for the seminar; in the ensuing twelve years, the authors worked together organizing the English and French programmes for the C.I.A.J.

In addition, they have presided over numerous conferences, workshops and discussions across Canada on the subject of decision writing, for the benefit of those engaged in that function: judges, administrators, arbitrators and referees.

This handbook is developed from one written for Francophones by Justice Mailhot, *Écrire la décision (Éd. Yvon Blais Inc. 1996).* Both are inspired by our experience at the seminars, exposed as we were to the superb quality of the American and Canadian professors who taught succeeding classes of judges. In large measure, the credit for any usefulness discovered here is to them, the errors to the undersigned. Though written with judges in mind, we hope the handbook will prove beneficial to everybody called upon to write decisions and even to those called upon to plead before the Courts.

The authors wish to thank in particular Professor James C. Raymond, professor of English at the University of Alabama, and all the dedicated professors whose knowledge of the subject, so generously shared, will have found its way, consciously or unconsciously, into these pages.

CHAPTER I

WHY WRITE A DECISION?

"Writing is a craft ... which you learn by writing," said Simone de Beauvoir. That's probably true, even for judges. However, the art of judging is something else again: it's not a craft, but rather an aptitude, almost an art. It is also a skill which is not given to everyone, made up of many ingredients such as the ability to reason and to express different shades of meaning, the ability to understand without necessarily accepting new ideas and concepts, and to appreciate the often contradictory arguments advanced by one side or another, before forming an opinion.

For over a decade now, judges, arbitrators and members of administrative boards have become increasingly aware of the importance of a well-written decision. After all, the parties to litigation are not the only consumers of judgments. Judges themselves are – of their own, and of other judges. Furthermore, we know to what extent judges have become prolific and know too well the increase in the number of pages created by writers of decisions since the arrival of the *Charter of Rights and Freedoms* in Canada.

It is therefore important to develop certain techniques in the writing of judgments to make them a pleasure to read and to write. For not all judges are natural writers. Some are blessed with remarkable writing skills, but many more arrive at a serviceable style only after a long and often painful gestation.

One does not learn how to write well by simply reading textbooks. Only repeated practice of writing, together with an awareness of the importance of effective communication, can lead to favourable results.

E.B. White described the process well[4]:

4. Quoted by Sophy Burnham in *For Writers Only*, Random House Canada, 1994.

> The main thing I try to do is write as clearly as I can. Because I have the greatest respect for the reader, and if he's going to the trouble of reading what I've written – I'm a slow reader myself and I guess most people are – why, the least I can do is make it as easy as possible for him to find out what I'm trying to say, trying to get at. I rewrite a good deal to make it clear.

Alexander Pope (1688-1744) said much the same:

> True ease in writing comes from art, not chance.
> As those move easiest who have learn't to dance.

Is there a single way, a proven formula for writing, be it a novel, an article for a magazine, or a decision? It seems not. All personal strategies are good, provided they reflect the personality of the author and unlock that author's creative energy, for all writing is, by definition, an act of creation.

Jeannine Étiemble, in a book on the art of writing published in 1970[5], assembled a number of texts of writers from around the world, dating from ancient times. She selected writings from Plato to Styron and passing through, Montaigne, Pope, Goethe, Poe, Sand, Faulkner, Hemingway, H. Miller and Moravia. Étiemble thus demonstrated that all of them developed over time the method which suited them best, which reflected their personality and responded to their interior voices of the moment.

The English writer, Samuel Johnson, managed to touch many bases in one short paragraph:

> Of composition there are different methods. Some employ at once memory and invention, and, with little intermediate use of the pen, form and polish large masses by continued meditation, and write their productions only when, in their own opinion, they have completed them. It is related of Virgil[6] that his custom was to pour out a great number of verses in the morning, and pass the day in retrenching exuberances and correcting inaccuracies. The method of Pope, as may be

5. Étiemble et Jeannine Étiemble, *L'art d'écrire*, Seghers, Paris 1970.
6. By Suetonius in his brief life of the poet.

> collected from his translation, was to write his first thoughts in his first words, and gradually to amplify, decorate, rectify, and refine them.[7]

Johnson himself told Boswell in 1766:

> When composing verses I have generally had them in my mind, perhaps fifty at a time, walking up and down in my room; and then I have written them down, and often, from laziness, have written only half lines... I remember I wrote a hundred lines of *The Vanity of Human Wishes* in a day.[8]

The conclusion of Étiemble finds confirmation in the observations of the following authors collected by Sophy Burnham[9].

JOHN BARTH:

> Like every writer's professional life, mine is spent doing a kind of dreaming – from the time I sit down at the desk and pick up my faithful fountain pen until the time I put the stuff on the Macintosh – which is a kind of waking up.

AGATHA CHRISTIE:

> All I needed was a steady table and typewriter. A marble topped bedroom washstand table made a good place; the dining room table between meals was also suitable.

TRUMAN CAPOTE:

> I am a completely horizontal author. I can't think unless I'm lying down, either in bed or stretched on a couch and with a cigarette and coffee handy.

RED SMITH:

> Writing is easy. All you do is sit staring at the blank sheet of paper until the drops of blood form on your forehead.

---

7. M.H. Abrams – Norton Anthology of English Literature – 5th edition 1987 – W.W. Norton & Cie, p. 1289.
8. Abrams, *op. cit.*, p. 2590.
9. Sophy Burnham, *op. cit.*

SINCLAIR LEWIS:

> Writers kid themselves – about themselves and other people. Take the talk about writing methods. Writing is just work – there's no secret. If you dictate or use a pen or type or type with your toes – it is just work.

* * * * *

For a Canadian perspective, who better than STEPHEN LEACOCK:

> You just jot down ideas as they occur to you. The jotting is simplicity itself – it is the occurring which is difficult.

As a co-owner of the political magazine *The Nation*, Paul Newman writes regularly for the magazine. But instead of using a computer like almost everyone now, he insists on the use of his old Smith-Corona typewriter. Apparently, he was never able to adapt to a computer because he longed for the ring of the warning bell at the end of a line.

It is therefore not surprising that Professor James C. Raymond titled his first book on writing: "Writing (is an unnatural act)".[10]

Judges face the same difficulty. Early in their careers they tend to set out in great detail the facts and legal principles to be applied. With time, the style becomes more personal, tighter, more concentrated. By comparing their first judgments with those written later, anyone can notice the change.

In time, all judges will develop their own style. "Practice makes perfect" applies to judgment writing.

Obviously, a judgment serves no one until it is issued. Once issued, it should be a pleasure to read and easy to understand. To achieve this objective requires an answer to the following questions – why write a decision and for whom?

---

10. *Writing (Is an Unnatural Act)*, Harper & Row, N.Y., 1980.

Although the outcome of a judicial process, a judgment is above all an act of communication. The *raison d'être* of a judgment is to settle a dispute. In addition, in crafting the decision which resolves the dispute, a judge must try to make it understood, if not accepted, by the losing party, by setting out the path travelled to arrive at the disposition. This intellectual exercise, this attempt to convince, is indeed an act of communication.

The quality of communication between writer and reader depends largely on the clarity of the style and its adaptation to the particular audience for whom it is intended.

Therefore it is important before starting a judgment to identify its potential audience, that is to say, who may read it? For example, is it a question of law or a question of fact? Is it a question of a class action where the result will apply to other similar situations or, is it a misunderstanding between individuals, unlikely to recur? Or again, is it an argument of a purely procedural nature, or rather a matter of interpretation to be given to a text of general interest?

On this preliminary determination will often depend the length of the text, the level of language, technical or general, and the organization of the judgment.

CHAPTER II

WHO READS THE DECISION?

For whom do judges write? For the parties and their counsel for a start. Of course. But if so, why recite at length the facts of the case and why repeat to the parties a story already too familiar? Why force oneself to a recitation of the facts if not to interest other readers, to whom the facts are unfamiliar and to explain to them the matters in issue and the result?

The potential audience for judgments includes several other readers. Among them: members of a panel when the court is a collegial one (judges, arbitrators, assessors), colleagues of the same court, board, or tribunal, members of the Bar, law professors, law students, similarly affected litigants, journalists who inform the public, and courts of appeal. To this mixture can be added, if rarely, the Supreme Court of Canada, other courts of last resort, and readers outside Canada. Indeed law reports, written or computerized, no longer know any limits – whether geographical, legal or linguistic.

Thus it must be recognized that the potential audience of a judgment is greater than that immediate audience made up of the parties and their counsel, themselves the first readers. The audience of a judgment is varied. The diversity of the audience changes from one judgment to another – it can be large or small depending on the type of decision. Nevertheless, this audience includes more than persons familiar with the law or with the facts of the case. Other readers, the public, are the "unknown witnesses" (George Sand).

It is therefore important to identify, if possible, the intended readers of each judgment. For example, a decision which flows from an unusual set of facts or a simple claim for an unpaid account does not speak to as wide an audience as a decision on a crucial social matter, on constitutional interpretation, or one that affects fundamental liberties in a new way, such as abortion, extradition, euthanasia, or Internet property rights.

Before starting to write, one must consider not only the message but also its recipient. Thus one will write for the intended reader, not for the sole benefit of the writer.

WRITING TO REACH THE INTENDED AUDIENCE

To reach these various audiences, while keeping in mind the objective of communication, may require some adaptation of language and style to each situation. Certain basic rules, however, may help to make the final text interesting to read and even to write. For it is important to those who must write regularly, to find some pleasure in writing in spite of the constraints and efforts which accompany the task. As it is difficult to foresee the useful life of a judgment – though admittedly most are short-lived – the primary reward to the writer rests in the pleasure of the writing process itself.

SOME BASIC RULES

1. Use simple and coherent language.
2. Avoid old-fashioned expressions and legalese.
3. Avoid the over-use of the passive voice.
4. Use a variety of short and long sentences and paragraphs.
5. Use connectives.
6. Explain sets of initials and acronyms.

1. Use simple and coherent language

The public is quick to reproach jurists, barristers, professors, judges, and arbitrators for using language that is too technical or even closed and for their failure to use everyday language in pleading or speaking. They are criticized for using a jargon known to them alone or to a few initiates.

Thus developed, first in the USA and then elsewhere, movements advocating "plain language", that is simple or everyday language[11]. Its proponents make themselves heard with considerable force. These movements for readability in English have their supporters and detractors. The trend, however, is irreversible. This does not require the adoption of a falsely simplistic style by the use of vulgarisms or common turns of phrase, but rather the choice of language that is natural, practical, and free from overaffected words and phrases. In short, we should write simply, taking great care in the choice of vocabulary.

No discussion of plain English is complete without reference to the difference between words of Anglo-Saxon origin and of Latin origin. For instance, the constant use of words of Latin origin in a text often produces a weaker prose. When words of Latin origin are combined with prepositional clusters as, "At this point in time..." (Now) or "Due to the fact that..." (Since, Because), sentences sink under their own weight. George Orwell made the point over 50 years ago when he rendered a well-known verse of *Ecclesiastes*:

> I returned and saw under the sun, that the race is not to the swift, nor the battle to the strong, neither yet bread to the wise, nor yet riches to men of understanding, not yet favour to men of skill; but time and chance happeneth to them all.
>
> in "modern English":
>
> Objective considerations of contemporary phenomena compel the conclusion that success or failure in competitive activities exhibits no tendency to be commensurate with innate capacity,

11. In Canada, the report of the Canadian Bar Association – Canadian Bankers' Association Joint Committee on Plain Language, *The Decline and Fall of Gobbledygook*, was adopted in 1991.

> but that a considerable element of the unpredictable must invariably be taken into account.[12]

Appendix I is a list of words of Latin origin, prepositional clusters, and other weighty words and phrases with suggested alternatives.

The last word on this subject should go to John Kenneth Galbraith[13], writing about economic prose in words applicable to judicial prose:

> I have always gained much help in writing in economics by the conviction that there is no idea associated with the subject that cannot, with sufficient effort, be stated in clear English. The obscurity that characterizes professional economic prose does not derive from the difficulty of the subject, but is the result of incomplete thought; or it reflects a priestly desire to differentiate oneself from the plain world of the layman; or it stems from the fear of having ones inadequacies found out. Nothing so protects error as an absence of readers or understanding.

2. Avoid old-fashioned expressions and legalese

Legal writing is one of those rare creations,
like the rat and the cockroach,
that would attract little sympathy even as an endangered species.

Richard Hyland
A defense of legal writing (1986)

When judges write, often, their greatest fault is their desire to appear learned when the emphasis should be to achieve simplicity and clarity. Lean and simple language hits the target better because it is better understood.

It is true that archaisms form part of the daily life of jurists; sometimes they represent a necessary link with the past and the

12. *Politics and the English Language* from *Inside the Whale and Other Essays*, Penguin, London, 1962.
13. *Writing, Typing, and Economics*, Atlantic Monthly, March 1978.

rules of ancient law, since the use of archaisms and latinisms has lasted for centuries. However, they are often unnecessary for present-day decisions and can usually be replaced by modern language.

In using technical terms to describe the simplest situations, judges and other decision writers have distanced themselves from the public. These terms, once commonly understood, are now barriers to understanding for many readers.

Thus, why use *viva voce, a fortiori* and *inter alia,* when *oral, all the more so,* and *among other things* do just as well?

Here is a short list for elimination and substitution:

- caveat emptor	*- let the buyer beware*
- de facto	*- in fact*
- ejusdem generis	*- of the same kind*
- et al.	*- and another (or others)*
- ex post facto	*- after the fact*
- fraus omnia corrumpit	*- fraud corrupts everything*
- inter alia	*- among others*
- nunc pro tunc	*- immediately*
- per curiam	*- by the court*
- primo, secundo	*- first, second*

Some Latin words are no longer thought of as Latin, but rather as English – *habeas corpus, affidavit, quorum.* Others are terms of art which have no synonym in ordinary English – *ex parte, mandamus, certiorari.*

Law's love affair with Latin over previous centuries can be explained by that language's precision when compared with the imprecision of developing English. Now that precision in English is attainable and comprehension of Latin, for most readers, is not – why continue the affair?

Therefore, current legal writing should avoid archaic words and legal jargon such as the following:

- Witnesseth
- Enter into a contract of sale
- Hereinabove mentioned
- Theretofore
- Thereunto appertaining
- To wit
- Thenceforth
- And/or
- Will and testament
- Here and above
- It is therefore ordered, adjudged and decreed

The same applies to the unpleasant legalese habit of using the expressions "the said" or "such" in judgments or pleadings:

Illustration (to be avoided)

It appears therefore that plaintiff at the time he purported to accept a mandate from defendant in respect of the said sale or exchange of her property was already the agent of the said Filler for the purpose of acquiring defendant's property with the right to claim a commission from the said Filler in respect of his services. There is, moreover, no evidence to indicate that the fact that plaintiff was acting under such a double mandate was ever disclosed to defendant.

Other Legalese: Numbers

In addition to old-fashioned words and latinisms which interfere with comprehension, the bad habit of writing numbers using both numerals and letters should also be eliminated to remove an additional obstacle to readability. That which many consider to be a legalism is not the exclusive prerogative of jurists; numerous documents exist, the product of engineers and surveyors, which deal with numbers in the same fashion.

Such habits were developed mainly to avoid error – to insure that a metes and bounds description was written precisely and without controversy in a deed of transfer, or in an official document which included a reference to a survey. The practice was extended to the writing of a cheque, and extended further when certain drafters exercising official functions were paid by the word. However, to write a decision today is neither to draw a cheque nor to describe the metes and bounds of a parcel of land. The proliferation of data and the need to read quickly combine to dictate an economy of words. In addition, to read a number written in numerals is always easier.

Therefore the following method of spelling out the date of a document should be abandoned:

> "The twenty-second day of November, One thousand nine hundred and ninety-three".

for simply: "November 22, 1993".

The most widely adopted rule for numbers is as follows: use words for numbers from one to ten (some authors say twenty) and use numerals for the higher numbers. Two exceptions to this rule: (1) when a sentence or a paragraph contains several numbers, one can write all the numbers in numerals, even when one of them is less than ten and (2) spell out numbers when beginning a sentence.

For sums of money, if there are no cents to be expressed, one can omit them as follows: $ 875 instead of $ 875.00.

Illustrations

To be avoided	To be adopted
The six (6) motions were heard simultaneously.	The six motions were heard simultaneously.
The three (3) plaintiffs submitted a total of twenty eight (28) grievances.	The 3 plaintiffs submitted a total of 28 grievances.
The property had frontage of 157 (one hundred and fifty seven) metres and a depth of 285.5 (two hundred and eighty five and five tenths) metres.	The property had a frontage of 157 metres and a depth of 285.5 metres.
The monthly rent is $ 541.00.	The monthly rent is $ 541.
76 members voted.	Seventy-six members voted.

3. Avoid the over-use of the passive voice

The active voice responds better to the attributes of the English language and encourages direct and apt expression. The passive voice, often heavy in English, dilutes the impact attained by the active voice. Here are several illustrations:

a) The wage rates of the part time employees were dealt with in the collective agreement.
The collective agreement dealt with the wage rates of the part time employees.

b) He was acquitted by the jury.
The jury acquitted him.

c) Evidence in support of the application for a rate increase was given by senior company employees and private consultants. Testimony during the hearing was presented in two phases. Senior company employees and private consultants testified in support of the application for a rate increase; this was done in two phases.

d) The witness is examined by the judge. The judge examines the witness.

e) It was reported by the doctor that the analysis was valid and accurate. The doctor said the analysis was accurate.

The difference in emphasis is clear. The active voice is stronger, more precise and communicates more effectively.

As always there are exceptions. When the subject is unimportant or unknown, choose the passive voice. "Trespassers will be prosecuted" is better than "We will prosecute trespassers"; who prosecutes is of no interest.

4. Use a variety of short and long sentences and paragraphs

A text composed of short sentences is easier to read; comprehension is simplified and communication facilitated. However, it is important to create some harmony in a text. A succession of short sentences often gives the unpleasant impression of a text which prattles and goes nowhere. Too many short sentences cause annoyance. On the other hand, an uninterrupted succession of long sentences suggests boredom. Nothing is more annoying than the task of concentrating on sentences both rambling and interminably long. The reaction is always the same: one jumps over the passage to the following paragraph, hoping to find a location more conducive to normal breathing and to comprehension. A series of sentences of identical length produces, like the continual ticking of a grandfather clock, an hypnotic effect. Variety in the length of sentences gives balance to a text and stimulates the reader.

In thinking of their audience, drafters of decisions will choose sentences of various lengths to create that desired rhythm which breathes life into a text. They will keep in mind the objectives of clarity and accessibility in granting to their readers periodic changes of pace.

Here are two extracts which illustrate the principle: one is from an opinion of the great American jurist, Benjamin Cardozo, the other the opening paragraphs of Katherine Mansfield's *The Garden-Party*:

> Danger invites rescue. The cry of distress is the summons to relief. The law does not ignore these reactions of the mind in tracing conduct to its consequences. It recognizes them as normal. It places their effect within the range of the natural and probable. The wrong that imperils life is a wrong to the imperiled victim; it is a wrong also to his rescuer. The State that leaves an opening in a bridge is liable to the child that falls into the stream, but liable also to the parent who plunges to its aid. The railroad company whose train approaches without signal is a wrongdoer toward the traveller surprised between the rails, but a wrongdoer also to the bystander who drags him from the path. The risk of rescue, if only it be not wanton, is born of the occasion. The emergency begets the man. The wrongdoer may not have foreseen the coming of a deliverer. He is accountable as if he had.

* * * * *

> And after all the weather was ideal. They could not have had a more perfect day for a garden-party if they had ordered it. Windless, warm, the sky without a cloud. Only the blue was veiled with a haze of light gold, as it is sometimes in early summer. The gardener had been up since dawn, mowing the lawns and sweeping them, until the grass and the dark flat rosettes where the daisy plants had been seemed to shine. As for the roses, you could not help feeling they understood that roses are the only flowers that impress people at garden-parties; the only flowers that everybody is certain of knowing. Hundreds, yes, literally hundreds, had come out in a single night; the green bushes bowed down as though they had been visited by archangels.

> Breakfast was not yet over before the men came to put up the marquee.

In these passages, the variety in the length of sentences and the rhythm which flows from it carry the reader forward; in the case of the short story by Katherine Mansfield, the atmosphere is intoxicating, the rhythm irresistible.

In contrast, a long sentence drafted without punctuation becomes laborious to read. Consider this example:

> Although the version of events of the accused is difficult to believe taking into account the fact among other things that it would be quite astonishing for a responsible father to let his children run about in a large department store at a moment when the store is jammed with shoppers and even in accepting the version of the accused that does not seem to be a contradiction of the version of the witness for the Crown that it was the accused himself who unpacked certain of the objects which the children had in their possession and who would have hidden them in the counters.

This text rewritten in three sentences is much clearer:

> That a responsible father would let his children run about in a crowded store is difficult to believe. Even if believed, the accused's testimony does not seem to contradict that of the witness for the Crown. She confirms having seen the father unpack certain of the goods which the children had in their possession and then hide them in the counter.

Paragraphs carry out the same function; they control the rhythm of reading and should make it easier. We have all had to read at one time or another decisions appearing in the old reported cases where the paragraphs go on for ever. Consider this 1952 example from Ontario, where the trial judge found it necessary to point out why the case before him did not square with the facts in other cases cited to him:

> In the light of these cases it is the duty of the Court to construe the contracts here in question and determine the duties of the engineer. These contracts contained no provision "that no sum

should be considered due nor should the plaintiff make any claim on account of any work executed by it unless the engineer of the corporation should certify the amount thereof and that the plaintiff is reasonably entitled thereto", with a general clause referring all disputes and differences to the final arbitration of the engineer, as in *Scott v. The Corporation of Liverpool, supra;* nor a clause similar to the one to which I have already referred, suggested by the Lord Chancellor in the same case; nor a clause that all differences were to be referred to the engineer, whose decision was to be final without giving reasons, as in *Roberts v. The Bury Improvement Commissioners, supra;* nor that the contractor would be paid when the engineer should have given his final certificate of approval, with an agreement that the decision of the engineer with respect to the quality and state of works executed and to the time within which they should have been executed should be final and without appeal and that any dispute between the plaintiff and defendant as to the value of any alteration or addition or concerning the true construction of the contract or anything relating thereto, the mode of deciding which was not otherwise expressly provided for, should be left to the determination and award of the engineer who might give a certificate instead of an award, as in *Jones et al. v. The President and Scholars of St. John's College, Oxford, supra;* nor that if any difference should arise between the defendant and the plaintiff concerning anything in connection with the contract, such difference should be referred to the engineer and his decision thereon should be final and binding on the plaintiff and the defendant, as in *Lawson v. The Wallasey Local Board, supra;* nor that the decision of the engineer on all matters relating to the work should be final and that payment should be made on the certificate of the engineer, as in *Hickman & Co. v. Roberts et al., supra;* nor that the payment should be made after the issue of a certificate of the engineer that the work had been satisfactorily carried out and on the issue of a certificate of another party of the amount due had been checked and found correct, as in *Panamena Europea Navigacion (Compania Limitada) v. Frederick Leyland & Company Limited (J. Russell & Company), supra.*

In the same vein, the following excerpt from an insurance contract requires either re-reading or re-writing to understand it:

> Option (b) – The new Policy may bear the same Policy-year Date as this Policy and be upon any plan of insurance being issued by the Company at the date hereof, except Term Insurance, in which case the premium thereon shall be the same as would have been payable had such new Policy been issued at the date of this Policy. Exchange for such a Policy shall be conditional upon the payment to the Company of the difference, with interest compounded annually at such rate not exceeding seven per cent, as the Directors may determine, between the premiums under this Policy, reduced by the premiums for any Disability Provision, and the premiums which would have been payable under such new Policy, reduced by the premiums for any Disability Provision provided, however, that if the premiums required for any Disability Provision be greater under such new Policy than under this Policy the extra amounts which would have been required, with interest as above stated, shall be payable to the Company in addition to the amount above stipulated. Any indebtedness on this Policy shall remain a charge on the new Policy.

Did you really read the above extracts? Probably not. Because, from the outset the reader concludes they would be of no interest, and moreover would be tedious. Nevertheless, some readers are required to scrutinize all the passages in judgments to understand them, to analyze them, to search for reasons to appeal, to compare them with other judgments, or to distinguish them.

Losing parties may never agree with a decision; they may be persuaded to accept it. Acceptance will come only if all parts of the judgment are accessible to the losing party.

Although the long paragraph written with the rhythm created by Katherine Mansfield (in the extract above) succeeds in stimulating the mind, short paragraphs permit readers to more easily get their bearings and to catch their breath, a useful advantage with a text both didactic and juridical. However, take care: an uninterrupted series of paragraphs of two lines will give readers the sensation of travelling in a car which stops abruptly every 50 metres. The reader may not only stop abruptly but fail to resume.

A variety in the length of paragraphs makes reading a more pleasant experience. The objective is diversity. Here is an example from the book of Simon Schama, *Dead Certainties*,[14] describing the moments before a guilty verdict:

> Not long after ten, one of these fellows in a cloth cap came bolting into the Lamb tavern shouting that the court was to reassemble at a quarter to eleven. The footsoldiers of the newspapers quickly mobilised themselves; not one grumbled at having to leave their mulled wine or porter.
>
> By ten-thirty the court-room was full again; overflowing in fact, the galleries jammed. The police had given up trying to shut the court-room doors, so another throng crowded at the rear all the way down the steps and into the street.
>
> Writing their memoirs (as many did), retired judges liked to refer to court-houses as "temples of justice". But the Boston Federal Court was more like the synagogue before the money changers had been cleared: a commotion of busy conversation and freely vented opinions. Over the eleven days of the trial, particular men and women who had sat in reserved places had become accustomed to each other's company, much as on a steamboat passage or a stage-coach journey. They had become familiar with the backs of those in front of them, their bonnet pins or collar studs; neighbouring spectators had obligingly alternated their elbows on the arm-rests of their chairs.
>
> Now they were reassembled, a nervous droning hubbub at a penultimate moment. But as soon as the Clerk of the Court announced a verdict had been agreed, all this noise abruptly stopped. So when John White Webster, with a ghostly pallor on his face, was led to his seat, he was faced with a sea of staring silent eyes.
>
> The jury came in and took, it seemed to everyone, an age shuffling to their seats; after them and with equal ponderousness, the bench.

14. A. A. Knopf, New York, 1991.

5. Use connectives

Connectives are single words or phrases which foreshadow the thought or idea to follow. They are essential in linking paragraphs or sections of a judgment, permitting the reader to anticipate the succeeding direction of the text. Often, a paragraph expresses an idea, a position, or a fact; to understand the relative position of the paragraph and to put it in its proper order, good writers use words and phrases which logically join or contrast two paragraphs, or which establish time, such as: *since, because, thus, nevertheless, moreover, however, in future, otherwise*, etc.

Illustration: For a more complete list of connectives and their uses, see Appendix II.

Most writers are familiar with sequential foreshadowing, such as *in the first place, first of all, following* etc., which helps in the logical development of a problem or a discussion. However, one must not abandon a reader in announcing an exposition of more than one part by the expression *first of all* and then forget to deal with at least the second part.

6. Explain sets of initials and acronyms

A set of initials of several words serves as an abbreviation and can form a word. It constitutes a useful shortening of words frequently used. For example, U.N., NATO, NAFTA, etc. These sets of initials have become part of the current language.

Conceived to make writing and reading easier, these methods of expression often become obstacles to communication or to the intelligent comprehension of text for those who do not know their precise meaning. Often, the context will reveal their meaning but if not, the intelligibility of the text requires writing the words in full before using a set of initials.

The following initials can identify organizations which carry a long name; this is an easy method to shorten a text, provided that the context will easily identify them:

UNICEF – United Nations International Children's Education Fund

CIDA – Canadian International Development Agency

O.M.B. – Ontario Municipal Board

N.B.I.D.B. – New Brunswick Industrial Development Bank

B.C.L.R.B. – British Columbia Labor Relations Board

The acronym, formed of initials or syllables of several words, is today an indispensable catch-all. It is defined as a set of initials written and pronounced as an ordinary word.

Radar – Radio detecting and ranging.

AIDS – Acquired immune deficiency syndrome.

Scuba – Self-contained underwater breathing apparatus.

The use of initials is a recent phenomenon and takes getting used to; over-using them, however, can affect adversely the intelligibility of the text.

* * * * *

To conclude, the basic rules examined above, often learned but often forgotten, exist for one primary purpose – to make texts easier to read. Readability is indispensable to effective communication of any message, including any judgment. Readability constitutes the key ingredient of communication between judges and their readers.

CHAPTER III

THE ORGANIZATION OF THE TEXT

The organization of the text is the difficult part of the task of decision writing. This process requires several hours to assemble the various elements of the puzzle, and to weigh and measure their relative value, several hours during which one reads and re-reads notes taken during the hearing, writes comments on the evidence, makes a summary of the testimony, and sets aside those parts of the evidence which appear at first glance irrelevant, but which may require a further examination. In addition, aspects of the relevant law will no doubt be added to the mix as they come to mind. Efficient writers undertake part of this preliminary work after each sitting of court; for example, it is good practice at the end of each day to write a short summary of the evidence, thus making the final task of fact-finding much simpler. The same applies to the reading of the case law and the pertinent texts.

Unfortunately, no one escapes the anguish of a blank page. Although writing is a constant part of the judicial function, decision writers regularly undergo a feeling of helplessness. This phenomenon seems inherent in the creation of a written text. Robert Badinter describes legal writing as follows[15]:

> Legal writing is thus a merciless exercise for jurists. The pen's resistance convinces them better than any critic of the incertitude of their reflection. [...] The written page is implacable. It reveals weaknesses, insufficiencies and confusion, those vices of thought which speech envelops and conceals. To speak the law is the mission of judges but to write the law is the true test of judges. More reason not to shy away.

As an antidote to the anguish of the blank page, consider the following advice by the American writer and teacher Natalie Goldberg[16]:

---

15. Translation of a text published in Le Point, no. 1000, Nov. 16, 1991.
16. *Writing Down the Bones*, Shambhala Publications Inc., 1986

> Okay. Your kids are climbing into the cereal box. You have $1.25 left in your checking account. Your husband can't find his shoes, your car won't start, you know you have lived a life of unfulfilled dreams. There is the threat of a nuclear holocaust, there is apartheid in South Africa, it is twenty degrees below zero outside, your nose itches, and you don't have even three plates that match to serve dinner on. Your feet are swollen, you need to make a dentist appointment, the dog needs to be let out, you have to defrost the chicken and make a phone call to your cousin in Boston, you're worried about your mother's glaucoma, you forgot to put film in the camera, Safeway has a sale on solid white tuna, you are waiting for a job offer, you just bought a computer and have to unpack it. You have to start eating sprouts and stop eating doughnuts, you lost your favourite pen, and the cat peed on your current notebook.
>
> Take out another notebook, pick up another pen, and just write, just write, just write. In the middle of the world, make one positive step. In the center of chaos, make one definitive act. Just write. Say yes, stay alive, be awake. Just write. Just write. Just write.

* * * * *

Choosing in which language to write (and even to take notes at the hearing) may perhaps be the first decision a writer will be faced with. In some jurisdictions, courts recognize two or more official languages. Bilingual and trilingual writers have a choice of taking notes and writing their decisions in one of them. When the parties to a dispute do not use the same official language, thought should be given early to the ultimate language of the decision, particularly where the facts involve specialized or technical terms.

However, this choice is reserved only for those writers who can express their thoughts fully and correctly, regardless of which language. If such is not the case, no choice can be made, and writers will use that language in which they can express every nuance necessary to the decision.

For those who are comfortable in more than one official language, write the decision in the language of the parties, where all use the same one. If the parties have used different official languages, write in the language of the losing party, remembering the importance for that party to understand why the suit was lost. The losing party will be in a better position to assess the wisdom of an appeal or possible settlement.

Another choice to be made by the writer of a decision is that perennial one of whether to use the first person or the third person. For those who are comfortable with a more formal tone, the use of the third person cannot be criticised. Care must be taken to be consistent throughout the text; do not refer to "the court" in one paragraph, and in another "the tribunal". Similarly, "the Board" in one line and "the Commission" in the next. To be avoided at all costs is the "we" that gives rise to the belief that a decision was written by several persons when the parties have seen only one at the hearing.

There is much to be said for a single trier of fact and law to use the first person singular. There can be no doubt that the opinion delivered is that of the person who heard the evidence, made the findings of fact and applied the law. Contrary to the practice in the province of Quebec, the use of the first person is not restricted to judges in an appellate jurisdiction, but is available to judges of the first instance in the common law provinces of Canada who find it appropriate to their personal style. To some, the use of the third person "the court" conveys the impression, particularly to the lay parties, of someone attempting to escape responsibility for hard decisions by interposing a non-personal, almost fictive, construct between what took place at the hearing and the author of the decision.

Arguably, there may be a difference between "I find the plaintiff went through a red light", and "The court finds the plaintiff went through a red light".

To others, the introduction of this personal note is not consistent with their perception of the formality and dignity that should accompany a judicial decision. In the final analysis, judges and other triers of first instance must choose that style most comfortable for them.

1. The title of proceedings and the identification of the parties

As with putting together a jig-saw puzzle, it is better to start with what seems to be the simplest.

Let us begin then, simply by drafting the title of proceedings or style of cause as is sometimes known. The way to do this varies slightly according to the customs established in each jurisdiction. A certain uniformity is desirable and probably will follow as a response to the imperatives of the information highway.

First, when to use the terms JUDGMENT, OPINION, DECISION, etc.? Do they mean the same thing? Not at all. Each has a specific sense:

Judgment:	The decision of a court of first instance, the decision rendered by a court of appeal or a court of last resort of a country. For example: the Court of Queen's Bench of Alberta, the Court of Appeal of Nova Scotia, the Supreme Court of the United States.
Opinion:	The reasons of each member of a panel of a board, a tribunal, or an appellate court.
Decision:	A generic term. Used to describe that which is decided by administrative boards and tribunals, as well as by courts.
Decree:	An act of administrative or ministerial authority of general import.
Verdict:	A finding of guilty or not guilty by a judge or jury.

The title of proceedings serves to group together on the first page all the basic preliminary information: the name of the jurisdiction, the place of the hearing, the date of the decision, the identity of the author, names and styles of the parties, and the nature of the matter.

The manner of setting out this information varies widely in the common law provinces in Canada and elsewhere, while still conveying most or all of the essential information noted above. These variations appear to be the product of long-standing conventions in particular locations, passed on from one judicial generation to another. Here follows a suggested model suitable for trial or appellate courts and administrative tribunals:

NAME OF COURT OR TRIBUNAL

	Date: April 29, 1998.
PROVINCE/STATE DISTRICT/REGION No: 131011-96 Hearing date(s):	Name(s) of Judge/Panel/Board member(s)
February 11, 1998 March 12 and 17, 1998	Madam Miriam Murphy (full address)______________________ Petitioner/Plaintiff Represented by: ________________ (name of Counsel/Attorney) **v.** The Township of Burnaby (full address) ______________________________ Respondent/Defendant Represented by: ________________ (name of Counsel/Attorney) **and** Mr. Peter Fitzgerald (full address)______________________ Third party / Intervenor Represented by: ________________ (name of Counsel/Attorney)

•JUDGMENT
•SUMMARY JUDGMENT
•SENTENCE
•ORDER

* * * * *

The golden rule in drafting a decision consists in getting down, on paper or on a screen, *immediately after the judgment is reserved*, a résumé of the facts and issues to be decided, adding the principal ideas that will form part of a conclusion. Even the best of memories can fail and pertinent details can rapidly fade. Of prime importance is to commit to this first exercise of drafting within 24 or 48 hours following the end of the submissions or the taking in reserve.

If your cases come one after another over several weeks or months, it is imperative to make a daily summary of the evidence, immediately setting out your impressions as to the pertinence of the evidence and the credibility of the witnesses. These impressions are never definitive and can later be changed. There is always a difference between the ideas which swirl around in your head and their placement in a structured order, a daily challenge for decision writers. Noting these ideas while they are still clearly remembered will simplify considerably the drafting of the final decision. Two contradictory forces are at play: first impressions are often the best, yet rarely is there writing without revision.

* * * * *

Before proceeding to a suggested plan, a preliminary question arises – how to refer to the parties?

Should we identify them by name, or by their status before the court as plaintiff, respondent etc.? From the point of view of the reader, a text gains considerable readability if one describes the individual parties by their names, with or without their first names, at the choice of the writer. The public (and many judges) easily loses itself in the labyrinth of nomenclature we know as the rules of civil procedure: the plaintiff – moving party – appellant; the defendant – plaintiff by counterclaim; the plaintiff – respondent in appeal; etc. The parties have names and an identity. Why not simply refer to them by name, instead of underlining the role they play before the court, thus forcing the reader to carry out laborious research?

Illustration:

Martin Edward O'Brien and Paul Jensen were jointly charged with possession of a narcotic for the purpose of trafficking. O'Brien was arrested and convicted; Jensen fled the country. Following O'Brien's conviction, Jensen returned to Canada. He told O'Brien's counsel, Mr. Simons, that he, Jensen, alone had committed the act. He agreed to testify to that effect. Before the hearing, Jensen died. Leave to adduce fresh evidence was obtained from the British Columbia Court of Appeal. Mr. Simons repeated Jensen's statement before that court. On the strength of Mr. Simons' testimony the court allowed the appeal and directed an acquittal. The substantial question upon which this Crown Appeal turns is whether Mr. Simons' evidence was inadmissible as hearsay.

Identifying the parties by their names helps the reader to more easily follow the evolution of this story involving several persons. Communication is enhanced. On the other hand, the following illustration tests the patience of the reader:

Illustration:

The defendants, plaintiffs by counterclaim, appellants, claim against the third party defendants by counterclaim respondents, in their capacity as executors of the late Geraint Patrice, a detailed report of the state of their administration of the estate, the defendants, plaintiffs by counterclaim, alleging against the latter negligence and delay.

Here is a possible compromise: use the names, while indicating once, at the beginning, their status before the court.

Illustration:

Donald Smith, plaintiff, was a passenger in a car driven by George Jones, defendant. The car failed to stop at an intersection and collided with a truck driven by Emily Harris, defendant. Alleging brake failure, Mr. Jones claims over against Acme Brake Specialists Limited, third party.

Can one use surnames only, or should the first names be included? When several persons have the same family name, as in family or testamentary matters for example, the inclusion of a first name is surely obligatory. In other circumstances, it is a question of personal style. Some decision writers, having once indicated the first name and surname of the parties are comfortable in identifying them by their surnames only in the subsequent text. Others, perhaps more conservative, find it discourteous, if not rude, to refer to them only by their last name. They meet their needs in this regard by referring to the individuals who appear before them as "Mrs." or "Mr." or "Ms.".

Corporations, municipalities, and governmental bodies can be described by using abbreviations, initials, or descriptive terms: the Crown corporation, the State agency, the board, the municipality, the corporation. However, it is important to guide the reader in setting out in full the name of the organization when it is first mentioned, adding in parentheses the set of initials or the chosen term to be used for each following reference to the organization. This technique is particularly useful when repetition of long names would deaden the text. Thus when one meets for the first time in a judgment an enterprise known as the Consolidated Carbolic Smokeball Limited (Carbolic), there is no doubt about how the company will be described in the following pages.

Illustrations:

1. This is a garnishment proceeding. Plaintiffs-garnishors, Reading & Bates Construction Company and Reading & Bates Horizontal Drilling, Limited (Reading), appeal the trial court's denial of their rule to traverse answers to interrogatories files by garnishee, Amerada Hess Corporation (Amerada). The trial court determined that Amerada answered Reading's interrogatories truthfully. The trial court also denied Reading's revocatory action against intervenors, LLR Holding Corporation (LLR) and

Baker Energy Resources Corporation (Baker Energy), ruling that Reading failed to discharge its burden of proving [...] that an April 22, 1992 security agreement between LLR and Baker Energy and [...]

2. BellSouth Advertising & Publishing Corporation obtained a judgment against Garfield & Associates for $36,576. Garfield was a customer of Security Bank. BellSouth served Security Bank with a writ of garnishment, seeking any of Garfield's funds that the bank was holding.

By convention, it is no longer necessary to use quotation marks, bold type or to add the words "hereinafter referred to as...", parentheses are sufficient.

When one person acts for another, it sometimes helps to understand the text to explain that the person has undertaken a proceeding having nothing to do with her as a private individual. Thus, a minister of government would be identified as "Madam A.B., in her capacity as Minister of the Environment", and thereafter as "the Minister".

*****

2. The plan

It is important to make a plan or outline of the decision beforehand and to follow it. Here is a suggested model:

PLAN

1. *Introduction:* *Describe briefly the situation before the court and answer these questions in two or three short sentences: who? did what? to whom? and what are the issues to be decided?*

2. *The narration of the pertinent facts:* by chronological order, or by description.

3. *Findings of credibility on the disputed facts.*

4. *Analysis:*

    a) the positions of the opposing parties;

    b) the comments of the judge and finding of facts;

    c) the application of the law to the facts as found.

5. *Conclusion.*

Having made a plan, several difficulties remain to be resolved. Here, in no particular order, are some of those difficulties and some suggestions for overcoming them.

3. A good beginning, or "the first paragraph says it all"

In terms of drafting, the beginning of a judgment is of enormous importance. It should accomplish several things: capture the interest of the reader, inform the reader of the object of the judgment, and provide a summary of the main issues.

To this end, begin by drafting two or three sentences which answer the following simple questions: *who* did *what* to *whom*? This should be followed immediately by a summary of the issues to be decided. The first paragraph or two thus form a preview of the judgment.

Unfortunately the opening paragraphs, too often, take the form of the minutes of the hearing, describing how the parties found themselves before the court and by which proceedings, rather than explaining what compelled them to litigate. As well, one often reads judgments which begin by: "This matter is a motion for divorce" [...] "This matter is a grievance on overtime" [...] "The court is seized of an application for a declaration ...", etc.

Such a sentence at the beginning of a judgment is often followed by a list of the various proceedings in the record and the exhibits filed, including secondary information such as the number of days of hearing by the court, the number of adjournments and their justification, the number of witnesses and their status, the date of service of the statement of claim, etc. Lamentably, two or three pages of the most tedious material. These bits of information which may turn out to be significant should not be found at the beginning of the judgment.

Avoid following these two examples:

1. The court is seized of two claims in damages, one the result of an alleged diversion of a water course, the other the negligent operation of a back hoe. The two actions were ordered to be heard together by Jeffries J. by order dated March 17, 1994, as the evidence is the same and concerns the same parties. Following the audience held on September 10, 1995 the parties were present. The court, having heard the evidence, reviewed the authorities submitted and deliberated thereon, now renders this judgment.

* * * * *

2. The appellant, T. C., was charged with and convicted of a violation of the *Retail Business Holidays Act*, R.S.O. 1980, c. 453, and in particular s s. 2(1), which reads as follows:

   "2.-(1) Every person carrying on a retail business in a retail business establishment shall ensure that no member of the public is admitted thereto and no goods or services are sold or offered for sale therein by retail on a holiday."

   In paragraph 1. (1)(a) of the Act, "holiday" is defined as follows:

   "1.(1)(a) "holiday" means:

   (i) New Year's Day,
   (ii) Good Friday
   (iii) Victoria Day,
   (iv) Dominion Day
   (v) Labour Day,

(vi) Thanksgiving Day
(vii) Christmas Day
(viii) Boxing Day
(ix) Sunday, and
(x) any other public holiday declared by proclamation of the Lieutenant Governor to be a holiday for the purposes of this Act;"

Both at the trial and on appeal, the Courts were informed that the circumstances were not in dispute. [. . .]

The opening paragraphs give the tone of a decision. The two preceding examples predict that the reading of these decisions will be painful. No-one mastered the art of beginning a judgment in a captivating manner more than Lord Denning, whether "bluebell time in Kent" or "a motorcycle scramble at Ipswich ...". Without necessarily imitating him, everyone is capable of an interesting beginning, of taking the care required when the facts or the type of litigation lend themselves to it.

Judges everywhere can do as well. Here are some beginnings of judgments which immediately capture the interest of the reader.

1- **Dickson J.** – On April 8, 1976 Teresa Taylor and a friend were taking a ski lesson from Paul Ankenman on the slopes of Gibson Pass, in Manning Park, British Columbia when Larry LaCasse came over the crest of a knoll and accidentally collided with her, causing her grievous injuries. Through her parents she sued LaCasse for skiing out of control, Ankenman for negligence in conducting the ski lesson, Jaegli Enterprises as Ankenman's employer, and other defendants as occupiers and operators of the ski hill for negligence in permitting a danger or trap to exist where Teresa was injured.

Compare with the beginning of the Court of Appeal decision:

Teresa Taylor, through her parents, sues to recover damages for tragic injuries suffered by her in a ski accident on

April 8, 1976, at Gibson Pass, in Manning Park, a Provincial Park in British Columbia.

The defendant Larry LaCasse accidentally collided with Teresa who had fallen in a course of a lesson that she and her friend Carol Williams were taking from a ski instructor, the defendant, Paul Ankenman.

The Taylors sue the defendant LaCasse alleging that he was negligent in skiing out of control when the accident occurred. They sue the defendant Ankenman in negligence for conducting the ski lesson without due regard for the safety of the two girls. They allege that Jaegli Enterprises Ltd. is liable as Ankenman's employer. They finally sue the remaining defendants as occupiers and operators of the ski hill for negligence in permitting a danger or a trap to exist through which Teresa was injured.

2- **Cory J.** – Theodore Steele, the respondent, has attained the age of 55. For almost 37 of those years he has been detained in an institution. In my view the issue raised on this appeal is whether the Parole Board erred in refusing to release him on parole with the result that his continuing imprisonment constitutes cruel and unusual punishment.

The period of incarceration has been long indeed. When the respondent entered prison, Mr. St. Laurent was Prime Minister and General Eisenhower was President. He remained incarcerated through the Cuban missile crisis, the assassination of President Kennedy, the Vietnam War, the F.L.Q. crisis, the Watergate scandal, the Iran/Iraq War, the easing of tension between the Soviet Union and the United States, and the enactment of the *Canadian Charter of Rights and Freedoms.* An era has passed.

3- **Burnett J.** – Idaho Code § 18-8002(4) provides that if a motorist "refuses" to take a blood-alcohol test after he has been arrested for driving under the influence, his operator's licence shall be suspended. Today we are asked to decide whether the test has been "refuse[d]" if the motorist initially declines the test but shortly thereafter agrees to take it.

As explained in more detail below, we hold that there is no refusal if the assent is still timely and is given unequivocally.

4- **Halvorson J.** – The plaintiff claims a real estate commission based upon a lease of the defendant's premises to a tenant found by the plaintiff. Groundwork for this litigation was laid when the commission arrangement was not reduced to writing.

There are two issues. Firstly, was there an oral agreement, and, secondly, if there was, is it enforceable notwithstanding the lack of writing?

5- **Picard J.** – The plaintiff, Debra McLaren, and the defendant Linda Schwalbe were driving motor vehicles which collided causing damage to the vehicles and injuries to the plaintiff. The issues in the case are: liability, including contributory negligence; general and special damages, including a claim for loss of wages and homemaking services.

6- Canada's first woman to be appointed a federal judge (1943) provides a fine example of who? did what? to whom? What are the issues to be decided?:

Kinnear Co.Ct.J. – This is an appeal from the conviction of the appellant at Cayuga on the 8th March 1956 by His Worship Magistrate T.G. Street under s. 110(1) of The Highway Traffic Act, R.S.O. 1950, c. 167, as amended by 1954, c. 35, s. 14, for failing to report an accident. There is no dispute about the facts. At about 10.30 p.m. on 24th February last the appellant drove a motor vehicle bearing licence number 476-749 for 1956 into the White Rose gas-station premises on Main Street in the town of Dunnville and his motor vehicle struck the gasoline-pump on those premises, causing it to catch fire. The damages occasioned by the collision amounted to approximately $400. The motor vehicle was entirely off the highway at the moment of impact. Immediately after the collision the appellant drove away with his car lights out, and he did not report the accident. He made full restitution after the charge had been laid against him.

The appellant pleaded not guilty and based his defence and this appeal on the ground that the accident occurred wholly on private premises and not on the highway. He maintained that s. 110(1) of The Highway Traffic Act applies only in cases where an accident is caused by a motor vehicle while it is on a highway, notwithstanding the fact that the words "on a highway" do not appear in the subsection.

7- **Beard J.** – In these written reasons, I am responding to two separate motions requesting the interpretation of two separate gifts contained in the will of Angeline Marie Blanche Charlesworth ("the testatrix"). As the issues raised in the motions are completely unrelated, I will deal with them separately, and I will refer to them as follows: Motion 1 – Gift to Family Members; and Motion 2 – Gift to Charity.

MOTION 1 – GIFT TO FAMILY MEMBERS

In her will, the testatrix made a gift of one-half of the residue of her estate to the following beneficiaries:

I direct my Trustee to invest and keep invested the other share of the residue of my estate in trust for the children of my niece. LYNNE ARBEZ, and my nephew, WAYNE KINDRET, in equal shares.

The issues to be determined by this court are as follows:

(i) Does the class of beneficiaries created by this gift include child conceived and born subsequent to the death of the testatrix?

(ii) If not, should the court approve a proposal to vary the gift to include such a child?

I have determined that these issues be resolved as follows:

(i) The class of beneficiaries created by this gift does not include a child conceived and born subsequent to the death of the testatrix; and

(ii) This court will approve the proposal to vary the gift to include the child who would otherwise be excluded and will consent to the variation on behalf of all minor beneficiaries. [...]

8- **Carthy J.A.** – The coined term "reverse sting" describes a police investigation using narcotics as bait to attract criminals with cash. The traditional approach of seeking to buy drugs using undercover agents works at the street level but only to the extent of attracting low-level dealers who are considered disposable by those further up the ladder. However, if a substantial quantity of narcotics can be offered for sale the upper-level dealers may become interested and not only expose themselves to prosecution, but also produce large sums of illicitly gained cash.

The primary question for resolution on this appeal is whether this police procedure is illegal and, if so, whether in this case, it justifies a stay of the prosecution of the two appellants who sought to pay undercover agents $270,000 for 50 kilograms of marihuana.

The appellants were convicted on two counts of conspiracy, one for trafficking in a narcotic, and the other for possession for the purpose of trafficking, after a trial before Madam Justice Caswell, without a jury. The appellant Campbell received a sentence of nine years and Shirose a sentence of six years. The appeals in each case are against both conviction and sentence. It is argued that the indictment is defective in so far as it charges multiple conspiracies; that evidence was wrongly excluded as protected by solicitor-client privilege; that hearsay evidence was improperly applied for its truth; and, more broadly, and I would say predominantly, that the entire police operation was an abuse of process justifying a stay of the prosecutions.

9- **Murphy J.** – All of the plaintiffs are or were sales representatives. The nature of their work and the terms of their employment involved them in calling at regular intervals on customers or potential customers scattered throughout wide areas usually involving four, five or more counties.

For all practical purpose the use of a motor car was essential to each of the plaintiffs in the course of his work. Every one of them was in fact provided with a motor car by his employer. In addition all of the employers concerned permitted their employees, including the plaintiffs, to use the cars so provided otherwise than for the business of the employer.

10- **Richard J.** – Malektoo Pootoogoo Alainga was a 34 year old Inuk when he died in Iqaluit on June 22, 1993. He had four dependent children at the time of his death. He died without making a will. He had, however, before his death designated two of his children as beneficiaries in life insurance policies which he had arranged through his employer Canadian Broadcasting Corporation. The administrator/administratrix of his estate applies to the court for an order pursuant to the *Dependants Relief Act,* R.S.N.W.T. 1988, c. D-4, directing that those designations of beneficiaries under the two life insurance policies are to be treated as testamentary dispositions for purposes of the *Dependants Relief Act.*

The circumstances of the four dependent children are as follows: [...]

4. The narrative of the pertinent facts

It is at this point in the drafting process where the importance of identifying the issues in the opening paragraphs surfaces.

Which should be set out first, the facts or the issues to be decided? Setting out of the facts is essential to the understanding of a decision and of the solution reached by the court. Nevertheless, facts are only useful in the context of the issues. It is useless to force the reader to remember unimportant facts which prevent a good understanding of the argument or which puts the reader on a false scent. Consequently, to ensure that only the pertinent facts will be recounted, the writer should first identify the issues. Readers will then easily decide which facts to retain and which to ignore while reading the narrative.

A long factual narrative at the opening of a judgment leaves the reader perplexed as to what may be ignored and what must be retained.

Consider the following set of facts:

1. On May 18, 1981 a train went off the tracks 20 kilometres North of Sudbury, Ontario.

2. In the adjoining forest, beavers had built a dam.

3. A colony of beavers had left the region during the summer of 1979.

4. The train was overcrowded.

5. The passenger, Peter Ferguson, was standing in the vestibule at the moment of the derailment.

6. He was grievously injured.

7. On May 20, 1982 he sued the owners of the train, a provincial company, for damages.

8. It rained heavily during the month of May 1981.

9. The dam suddenly collapsed and 7,200,000 gallons of water flooded the rail bed, and washed away the tracks.

If the issue to be decided is the failure to meet a limitation date, facts no. 1, 6 and 7 are sufficient.

If it is necessary to determine whether the accident was due to unforeseeable circumstances, facts no. 1, 2, 3, 8 and 9 must be examined.

If it is a question of contributory negligence, facts no. 1, 4, 5 and 6 are pertinent.

On the other hand, if the court must fix the damages to be awarded, the facts as set out are insufficient. Statement no. 6 is quite laconic. It does not tell the nature and the extent of the injuries, the permanent incapacity, if any, the lengths of stay in hospital, the number of operations, the degree of pain and suffering of the victim and his family, the length of his convalescence and recovery. The narration of the facts would need to be expanded.

It follows that the issues to be decided should be identified and set out before the **detailed** narration of the facts, forcing the drafter to include only those facts essential to the litigation. Of course, it is for the lawyers to put in evidence more facts than less, but it is up to the judge to prune them.

Illustrations:

1. THE COURT – The issue in this appeal is the validity of an interlocutory injunction prohibiting Chantal Daigle from having an abortion. The injunction was granted at the request of Ms. Daigle's former boyfriend, Jean-Guy Tremblay. Because of the urgency and importance of the case, Ms. Daigle being some 21 weeks pregnant at the time, the Court agreed to hear the application for leave to appeal, and then heard the appeal itself, on short notice during the Court's summer recess. According to the medical evidence, generally no hospital centre in the province of Quebec would permit a voluntary abortion after 20 weeks of pregnancy; patients would be required to go to the United States if they wished to terminate a pregnancy after 20 weeks, each week adding to the surgical risk. A decision in the appeal was delivered from the bench on the day of the hearing, August 8, 1989. The Court was unanimous in the view that the appeal should be allowed. It was also stated that the reasons for the decision would be rendered at a later date. The following are those reasons.[17]

2. Is an individual who has been found guilty of an offence in Ontario denied the right to the equal protection and the

17. *Tremblay* v. *Daigle*, [1989] 2 R.C.S. 530, 535.

> equal benefit of the law without discrimination if he is subject to a harsher penalty prescribed by law than an individual who in like circumstances is found guilty of the same offence in certain other provinces of Canada or in the Northwest Territories?
>
> That is the principal issue which arises in these appeals. The subsidiary issue is what is the appropriate remedy if there has been a denial of that right.

Usually, the facts are developed in chronological order. This is more logical and easier to follow for people who know nothing of the events which brought the parties before the court. Ordinarily, events take place in a certain order and their presentation to the reader in that same order will render them easier to absorb.

Although essential, the narration of the facts should not become an annoying accumulation of useless details. To tell a story of events leading to a law suit does not mean to create an inventory. Choose the events necessary to the good development of the narrative and organize them in an interesting way.

Here is an interesting recital of unusual facts:

> **Denning J.** – To some this may appear to be a small matter, but to Mr. Harry Hook it is very important. He is a street trader in the Barnsley market. He has been trading there for some six years without any complaint being made against him; but, nevertheless, he has now been banned from trading in the market for life. All because of a trifling incident. On Wednesday, October 16, 1974, the market closed at 5:30. So were all the lavatories, or "toilets" as they are now called. They were locked up. Three-quarters of an hour later, at 6:20 Harry Hook had an urgent call of nature. He wanted to relieve himself. He went into a side street near the market and there made water, or "urinated", as it is now said. No one was about except one or two employees of the council, who were cleaning up. They rebuked him. He said: "I can do it here if I like". They reported him to a security officer who came up. The security officer reprimanded

> Harry Hook. We are not told the words used by the security officer. I expect they were in language which street traders understand. Harry Hook made an appropriate reply. Again we are not told the actual words, but it is not difficult to guess. I expect it was an emphatic version of "You be off". At any rate, the security officer described them as words of abuse. Touchstone would say the security officer gave the "reproof valiant" and Harry Hook gave the "countercheck quarrelsome": As you Like It, Act V, Scene IV.
>
> On the Thursday morning the security officer reported the incident. The market manager thought it was a serious matter. So he saw Mr. Hook the next day, Friday, October 18. Mr. Hook admitted it and said he was sorry for what had happened. The market manager was not satisfied to leave it there. He reported the incident to the chairman of the amenity services committee of the council. He says that the chairman agreed "that staff should be protected from such abuse." That very day the market manager wrote a letter to Mr. Hook, banning him from trading in the market.

The description of a location, a house, an object, is seldom subject to any particular rule. One can describe a room from the entrance to the exit, from the ceiling to the floor, from the exterior to the interior, from the general to the particular, or the opposite. One can also linger over the description of its brightness, its location, its atmosphere, its cleanliness, its scent, its decor, etc. All this depends only on whether the author wishes to emphasize one aspect rather than another.

Illustration:

> The lights were dim and smoke filled the large room. From the entrance, one could see the red colour of the walls in full contrast with the whiteness of the tablecloths. No carpet covered the old-wooden floor.

In an *appeal* judgment, select the facts extremely carefully. Readers will better determine then if the judgment has application to other fact situations.

5. Findings of credibility on the disputed facts

First, make a *summary* of the oral testimony. Avoid describing at length the responses of each witness to the innumerable questions put by the lawyers in examination-in-chief, cross-examination or reply.

Examinations of witnesses are often lengthy and slow. Witnesses are generally summoned to appear to establish precise facts; that understood, the judge should, for each witness, capture the essential fact or the determining response for the solution to the dispute.

Moreover, it is not necessary to make a list of the witnesses. It is enough to identify the undisputed facts and make findings of those in dispute, all within the rubric of pertinence. It is important to make findings of credibility when establishing the probative force of a witness' testimony, and to give reasons. Regardless of any jurisprudence to the contrary, a party or witness deserves to know why his testimony is not accepted.

Illustration:

> The accused testified he was standing on the corner, when someone unknown to him thrust the stolen television set in his hands, and ran off. Nothing in his manner or demeanour suggested he was trying to deceive the court.
>
> However, his testimony was not consistent within itself. Even in examination-in-chief, he contradicted himself, while in cross-examination, counsel for the Crown established many inconsistencies in his story.
>
> Moreover, his evidence is inconsistent with the uncontroverted facts and ordinary life experience. No one at the busy corner saw the events he described; persons do not normally thrust television sets into another's hands.
>
> I reject the accused's evidence.

However, diatribes against a witness are not useful, save in the rarest of cases.

6. The analysis

The best way of organizing all the submissions is to summarize the positions taken by each party on each issue to be resolved. These issues will have been identified in a succinct fashion at the beginning of the judgment. In this part of the judgment, the examination of the litigious questions is to be done in a logical order: for example, the existence of negligence, causation of injury, contributory negligence and damages for the injury. Many times, the necessity of setting out both positions on any issue can be avoided; if the plaintiff is in favour of a proposition the reader can usually infer the defendant is against it.

Illustration:

> Mrs. Keenan says that Mr. Drew's negligent left turn into her lane caused her to swerve and strike the tree. The impact broke both her legs, resulting in general damages of $150,000 and special damages of $27,532.60.
>
> Mr. Drew says Mrs. Keenan's failure to keep a proper lookout makes her solely responsible for the accident.

If there are several issues to discuss, begin with the one whose solution will govern all others, leaving aside the other issues raised. Sometimes, each of the questions require consideration: one choice is to treat them in the same sequence as that followed by counsel, or start with the issue most easily resolved, proceeding towards the more difficult. Indeed, this process can be reversed; there is no rule that requires one approach over another.

There is but one obligation: to correctly describe the arguments in support of each party's position on each issue, and to give clear reasons justifying the result. Whether the judge decides in favour of one party's position or another, the reasons given must be both clear and concise.

The word "justifying" is chosen with care. One could object and say that judges don't have to justify anything. Nevertheless, reasons are the foundation of the result, a form of justification. We submit judges must give reasons for their decisions, regardless of any suggestion to the contrary in the jurisprudence. To do otherwise is to write a bad decision. Whether the conclusion is reached by inductive or deductive reasoning, the process resembles a form of justification different from that used by counsel in argument. Counsel must convince in order to succeed; judges are not required to convince, but rather to make themselves understood. They must therefore express their reasons in a fashion that will carry with them the support of the majority of the readers. The losing parties may never be convinced their cause was wrong but they are entitled to know why they lost and how the judge reached that result.

* * * * *

Sub-titles

When a decision is particularly long, the careful (sparing) use of sub-titles can simplify the text and facilitate the location of specific issues examined. With a judgment of two dozen pages or less, it should not be necessary to guide the readers other than by the logical sequence of ideas. For an example, see the system used by Dickson C.J.C. in *Hunter et al v. Southam Inc.*, [1984] 2 S.C.R. 145. See also: *Briffett* v. *Gander and District Hospital Board et al.* (1996), 137 Nfld. & P.E.I.R. 271 – and *K. (W.)* v. *Pornbacher* (1997), 32 B.C.L.R. (3d) 360.

7. The conclusion

There are two schools of thought. One favors giving the result at the end of the judgment, the other at the beginning?

Traditionally, judges give the result at the end of their reasons, after having set out in great detail the facts, the issues to be decided, the submissions presented by the various parties, the various premises which underlie their reasons, and their progression towards the final result. The length of the reasons depends on the number of issues to be decided, their difficulty, the complexity of the facts and the law, the personality of the judge, and his or her style of reasoning and writing; during this process, the readers wait with heightened expectation. Consciously or unconsciously, they try to predict the result of the dispute and guess what the conclusion will be – often with mixed success, sometimes with astonishment. This is the style of Alfred Hitchcock or Agatha Christie: keep the secret of the ending as long and as well as possible to keep the readers in suspense.

This school of thought has its detractors. We all know that most readers of judgments first turn to the last page to read the judge's conclusion. Only then does there follow a complete reading of the judgment. So much for the element of surprise! Moreover, anyone reading a published decision will begin with the headnote, removing thus any possibility of surprise.

Therefore, although the conventional method of retaining the result to the last has the merit of following the logic of the argument and satisfying the requirements of deductive reasoning, the idea of concealing the result until the end is a fiction. Consequently, nothing prevents one from setting out, at the beginning or very early in the text, the result of the decision. It will fall to each writer to adopt one method or the other, according to the nature of the judgment. Thus, in a judgment bearing on the custody of a child it is perhaps better to say early on to whom the court will entrust custody; in such a circumstance the suspense is often painful, given the emotions always present. On the other hand, a decision bearing on a single question of law lends itself more easily to syllogism and deduction in its pure form, the result flowing from the enunciation of the underlying premises.

The judge can choose which strategy to adopt, according to the circumstances. If, in order to gain acceptance by the readers, it is necessary to persuade them, better to follow a gradual progression, guiding them gently towards the conclusion. The author will then let fall here and there subtle hints, like the little white stones dropped by design by Tom Thumb.

In sum, one can choose either to announce the result at the beginning or at the end; if the latter, let the audience guess the result early on in the judgment.

Whatever the choices, the reader must be persuaded of the wisdom of the result.

The result must reflect two important characteristics: brevity and directness expressed in the active voice. The conclusions of a judgment should be executory, as they aim to settle the litigation; it is key they be expressed with determination, precision, and in an affirmative manner.

Thus, one replaces a disposition expressed in the passive voice:

(a) For these reasons, the motion is denied or is not granted with costs.

(b) For these reasons, the grievance is declared out of time.

by the active voice:

(a) For these reasons, the court denies the motion with costs.

(b) For these reasons, the arbitration Board declares the grievance out of time and dismisses it.

Avoid such expressions as "I believe the action should be dismissed", "I think the plaintiff must succeed", "the defendant should bear the costs", and other expressions which dilute the vigour which should characterize the result.

CHAPTER IV

CONCISENESS

Brevity is the soul of wit.

Alexander Pope

Whoever reads the law reports of more than 30 years ago will rediscover the sense of the word "concise". These decisions contain hardly more than a few pages, often only one for procedural issues. Brief they may have been, precise they usually were.

What has happened in the legal world? Several factors have contributed to inflation: the rupture of social boundaries, the proliferation of laws, the advent of charters of rights and freedoms which followed the abuses of World War II, the multiplication of jurisdictions, and the accelerated development of technologies such as the photocopier and computer-driven communication. This combination has had its effect on judicial writing.

Sooner or later, this inflation, this prolixity, should be controlled.

Human beings still have only 24 hours a day to enjoy. Members of the public no longer have access to decisions which affect them, because those decisions have become too long and too complicated to read, never mind understand.

We must change our ways or change will be forced upon us. There already exists a limit on the number of pages for a factum in appeal courts. Very soon similar restraints could be imposed on pleadings and on judgments, with obvious exceptions where warranted.

Brevity does not mean, however, exemption from giving reasons. Reasons are essential to communication and to understanding. As Justice Estey puts it[18]:

> Brevity in this era of prolixity is commendable and might well be rewarded by a different result herein but for the fact that the order of the Board reveals only conclusions without any hint of the reasoning process which led thereto. For example, none of the factors which the Board took into account, in reaching its conclusion that the amounts contested were not "past losses" are revealed so that a reviewing tribunal cannot with any assurance determine that the statutory mandates bearing upon the Board's process have been heeded.

The adoption of a concise style remains a primary objective of judgment writing – the fewest words possible, as simply as possible.

SOME PRACTICAL ADVICE TO SHORTEN DECISIONS

1. Avoid reproducing the pleadings, the factums (if any) and extracts from the testimony of witnesses

The aim of any argument being to convince, the pleadings and factums are deliberately repetitive. Decisions should not repeat them, but rather summarize or paraphrase them.

Illustrations: (to be avoided)

1. The plaintiff was instructed to take the tractor back to St. Paul Sales, and it was tied up for seven or eight days while repairs were effected, again under warranty. At this particular time of the year, the plaintiff stated, he needed the heavy tractor to plough snow to reach his haystacks in the field as he required hay supplies to feed approximately 120 head of cattle that he had at the time.

18. *Northwestern Utilities Ltd. and others* v. *Edmonton*, [1979] 1 R.C.S. 707.

On 8th February 1971 the plaintiff was still experiencing difficulties with the hydraulic system and took the tractor back to St. Paul Sales, where one of the hydraulic lines was replaced and the unit was again tied up for a couple of days. The plaintiff stated that he was surprised at the number of problems he was experiencing with the new tractor as he had not had any similar problems with previous Massey-Ferguson tractors and had maintained the 1100 unit in the same fashion as he had looked after the previous units.

He said that from previous experience he would have expected the new tractor, with the amount of use it was receiving, to go for five or six years without any major tie-up for repairs or replacements. The plaintiff admitted that when the 1100 was working satisfactorily it performed the jobs he required it to do but that he was unable to count on it being available on a consistent basis when he needed it. At the time when the plaintiff acquired the 1100 he also acquired a heavier cultivator which was too large to be operated with his older, smaller tractor.

The plaintiff also stated that in early 1971 he noticed it was taking St. Paul Sales longer than usual to get spare parts for the 1100. He particularly remembered that they had ordered spare parts to repair the steering assembly, and that it took from December 1970 to May 1971 before delivery, and that then the wrong part was received and had to be re-ordered, necessitating a further delay. On 6th June 1971 St. Paul Sales effected some temporary repairs to the steering, tying up the tractor for two days during spring work. In the middle of July 1971 the temporary repairs proved insufficient, and the 1100 was again brought into St. Paul Sales and tied up for another three days. The plaintiff alleges that the breakdowns in the tractor and the resulting tie-ups in the spring of 1971 made it impossible for him to complete his seeding, and as a direct result of this problem he left 200 acres, which he had intended to cultivate and seed to barley, unseeded. He stated that he tried to obtain another tractor or rent other equipment at that time to do the preparation work and seeding but all the equipment in the area was already committed and none was available. At this point all the plaintiff had available himself was a small Massey-Ferguson tractor and a large cultivator that was too big for the small tractor to pull.

[...]

During this period, the plaintiff alleges, he tried everywhere in the area to borrow or rent equipment but none was available. He stated that he also asked Massey-Ferguson and St. Paul Sales for the loan of a unit but that Massey-Ferguson said it had none available, and that St. Paul Sales was in the process of going out of business and had no suitable unit to loan to the plaintiff.

2. This appeal is from a judgment of Mr. Justice Raney, of the 12th July, 1929, dismissing the action without costs.

The action was for damages occasioned at the village of Colborne, on the 24th September, 1928, about 4:30 p.m., when a collision occurred on the provincial highway between two Ford cars, one driven West by the plaintiff's husband, and the other east or north-east by the defendant. The plaintiff, accompanying her husband, was seriously injured and claimed $15,000 damages.

Among the several grounds of negligence charged, the most material is:

"(e) The defendant suddenly, and without any warning or regard for the on-coming traffic, altered the direction in which he was travelling, by endeavouring to turn into a lane at the North side of the said provincial highway, and, in so doing, struck the motor-car in which the plaintiff was driving, and caused the said injuries to the plaintiff."

The defence was that Usher, after giving due notice, had started to turn towards a lane on the North side of the highway, and was barely moving when the car in which the plaintiff was travelling came along at a speed of 50 or 60 miles an hour, and was driven by her husband into the defendant's car, injuring him and damaging his car. Negligence on the part of the defendant was denied, and a settlement with the plaintiff's husband pleaded, thus:

"4. The defendant further says that at the time of the accident, because of the ill-health of the wife of the defendant, who was leaving the following day for Plymouth, Michigan, with the defendant, to consult a physician there, the defendant and the plaintiff's husband, as representing himself and the plaintiff, came to an agreement with the defendant for the defendant to pay the damages to the car driven by the plaintiff's husband, in full settlement of all claims of every kind and description, and which sum was paid prior to the institution of this action, and the plaintiff pleads such settlement as an answer and bar to the plaintiff's action."

The following re-count of arguments between counsels is much easier to read:

Murphy J. – This is an application by the plaintiffs for an order for further and better discovery to be made by the first fourteen defendants. As counsel for the plaintiffs had occasion on the opening of the motion to refer to a document which the defendants contended was privileged, a preliminary point arose.

On behalf of the plaintiffs it was argued that even if the document was privileged (and this they deny), its existence should have been disclosed by the defendants in the affidavit of discovery sworn by them and, if appropriate, privilege claimed for it in that affidavit.

To that argument counsel on behalf of the defendants replied as follows: that such was the nature of the privilege attaching to the document in question that they were entitled to confidentiality in respect of the very existence of the document. For that proposition reliance was placed on the decision of the House of Lords in *Rush & Tompkins Ltd. V. G.L.C.* [1989] A.C. 1280.

As already indicated, it is useless to reproduce the testimony of witnesses as given: a summary is sufficient although, in exceptional circumstances, it may include a word for word transcription of a specific answer. Far too familiar are the long pauses, the meanderings, the hesitations and the repetitions which often characterize examination-in-chief and cross-examination punctuated with objections by counsels. Their reproduction makes the reader's task exceedingly dreary.

Illustration: (to be avoided)

On his cross-examination this witness said:

"I had not discussed this matter with Louis before we went to his house. He did not show any surprise. I did not conclude that anything had taken place between the two of them. Theodore had told me the conditions he wanted. I don't know that he told me that Louis was agreeable. I knew he was not parting with all his property, because he had other property at Corner Brook, vacant land. I would not give more than two thousand dollars for the property. I asked him if there were any encumbrances on the property, and he said there was no will and there were no encumbrances on the property. I knew this was really the larger portion of Theodore's estate. He said "I'm getting old now and am not feeling very well these days and I would like to have someone look after me in my old age". He said he wanted to pass over all his property to Louis, that he would like Louis to look after him in case he got sick, to be able to feed and clothe him in case he got in financial straits. I asked him did he want to be furnished with a doctor. He said 'Yes, if I need a doctor or nurse to look after me'. I do think that the three buildings that Theodore owned were together as valuable as the one that Louis owned. I explained the nature of the deed. I did not point out to Theodore that a will might serve his purpose better. I thought he was disposing of his property, and that he was disposing of it to his own satisfaction. He said it was Louis' now when the document was completed. I must have used the word 'demise' inadvertently. It should be 'convey' as well as 'demise'. I did not explain any particular words, nor did I explain what would happen if Louis had failed to support and maintain Theodore. I explained the effect of the deed to him. I sent the deed on for registration at the request of Louis, who paid me the registration fee of three dollars. I knew that an order for support had been made by the magistrate. I learned this from the magistrate. This conveyance was made after that."

What a witness said can be recounted simply.

Illustration:

In early December 1994, the doctor took the cast off and told him to take it easy for another week. Then the plaintiff was released to go back to work.

On cross-examination, he stated that during the period of his disability, he worked at odd jobs mostly for food.

Anthony Blanchard testified that he was plaintiff's supervisor at Colt. At the end of the day in question, he drove the truck out of the vehicle gate at the work site and picked up the men whom he usually drove to the ferry.

In criminal matters, it is unnecessary to quote the text of the information or the indictment, unless the document itself is in issue. Often, indictments contain several counts, whose reproduction is painful to read. Thus, particularly at the beginning of a judgment, it is better to describe the nature of the charge in a few words.

Illustration:

Write: Charged with first degree murder, the accused was tried by judge and jury.

Instead of: The accused in the instant case was tried before the undersigned judge, at which time he responded to the following charge:

At Toronto, in the province of Ontario, on or about the 31st day of July 1995, illegally and voluntarily did cause the death of George Jones, and did thereby commit murder in the first degree, contrary to article 231(2) of the Criminal Code.

One can describe a charge in easy and understandable language.

Illustrations:

(1) **Laskin J.A.** – A fight in the early morning hours of January 11, 1990 ended in the death of Clive Brown. During the fight the appellant Eric Jenkins struck Brown on the head with a hammer; his twin brother, the appellant Everett Jenkins stabbed Brown with a knife six times. Two of the knife wounds were fatal.

Eric and Everett Jenkins were charged with first degree murder. The Crown's theory was that the two accused deliberately attacked Brown – to retaliate for an incident hours earlier in which Brown had badly injured Eric Jenkins. Both accused pleaded not guilty. Their defence was self-defence. Everett Jenkins testified; Eric Jenkins did not.

(2) The accused is charged with impaired driving.

2. Have the courage to select only the essential facts and to discuss solely the real issues

As we have already seen, judges should strive to include only what is necessary to the understanding of the facts and the development of a solution. To quote Beetz J.[19]:

> The judge is bound by the issues before him and does not extend his ruling beyond what is necessary to settle them.

Set aside personal opinions. The following extract from an old decision makes the point:

Illustration: (to be avoided)

> Before he entered into the present, and only marriage, he had already fathered a daughter (now 17 years old) in Jamaica. That child now lives in Chicago and Mr. Francis says that he has a duty to contribute to her support. He has also fathered a son as a result of the adulterous union which has formed the basis of this action for divorce. Mr. Francis has either been uncommonly unfortunate in, or monumentally indifferent to, the practice of birth control. I also find the recently manifested concern for the support of his teenage daughter rather unconvincing. Whatever may be his social or moral obligation towards these other two children, there are no outstanding court orders against him requiring him to support either of them.

Avoid writing a thesis on a particular subject, leaving this task to university professors, even where the temptation is great because of interest in the issue. Resist the temptation to flog the main issue to death, or to drag the reader into subsidiary issues having no connection with the thrust of the judgment.

19. Supreme Court of Canada's Justice (1927-1991) in *Compagnie Immobilière Viger* v. *L. Giguère Inc.*, [1977] 2 R.C.S. 77.

3. Reduce citations and shorten the quotations

Those who borrow clothes confirm the poverty of their wardrobe.

Max Jacob

What to cite

Confine yourself to the binding decisions or the persuasive ones, such as the judgments of the Supreme Court of Canada or the Court of last resort in a country. It is useless to touch on all the decisions rendered by various jurisdictions on a given subject, unless you are writing a doctoral thesis, something a judgment should not be:

> It is undesirable to cumber a judgment with all the apparatus of research which Bench and Bar have utilised in ascertaining the principle of law to be applied.[20]

What to quote

Judges quote too often and too much. Why do we quote so much? Because we feel it makes us look wise? To parade one's knowledge? Because it's faster to quote in detail what others have written, rather than summarizing its essentials? Quotations should be used as guides, not crutches. They serve no purpose if read perfunctorily, or not at all. Why do we skip over them? Because it is often difficult to know what purpose they serve and more difficult to dig out the truly pertinent part. They are like a series of ingredients set down one after another without having made clear the actual link to the essential issue.

And yet, the applicable rule of law is often quite clear and quite well known, thanks to its clear expression in the statute itself.

How to quote

When it is necessary to quote, reproduce only the essential part of the text which illustrates your point. Introduce the quota-

20. Lord Macmillan – *The writing of judgments*, (1948) 26 C.B.R. 498.

tion by paraphrasing so that the quoted text is more accessible to your readers. When one paraphrases a quotation to follow, it gives the hurried reader an opportunity to jump over the text quoted while still retaining the train of thought of the author.

Finally, emphasize the important words or the key sentences. Emphasis captures the attention and helps to imprint the passage into the mind of the reader.

Illustrations:

1. In *Shell Canada v. Travailleurs Unis du pétrole*[21], J. Chouinard J. concluded that an arbitrator has exclusive jurisdiction over a claim for damages for the violation of a labour collective agreement:

   > In view of *Brunet (supra)* and *Imbleau (supra)*, and for the reasons stated, therefore, I conclude that in a case like the one at bar, in which respondents are sued for **damages for the violation of clauses** in which they had undertaken there would not be a strike, **the matter constitutes a grievance within the jurisdiction of the arbitrator**. [Emphasis added]

   (To be faithful to the text quoted, when something has been brought to the attention of the reader by underlining, the words [emphasis added] in brackets should be added at the end of the quotation.)

2. Any request for instruction or assistance from a jury must be treated carefully. However, in the case where a jury wishes to have evidence read or played again, problems can arise, especially in procedural fairness. In *R.*. v. *Wydryk* (1971), 5 C.C.C. (2d) 473, it was noted that "when some particular area of a witness' evidence is read at a jury's request, it is incumbent upon the trial judge to see that all the evidence pertaining to that area is included – else an unfair and biased result might

21. [1980] 2 R.C.S. 181, 188.

> appear" (p. 480). This was the problem faced by the trial judge.

Note that the former practice of referring to a judge with the title "Honourable", or the adjective "learned", is no longer necessary today, no matter how authoritative the opinion or the judgment is. To quote the opinion of a particular judge, write simply "In the case of XYZ, Carson J. wrote", "On appeal, Featherson J.A. said", or "Justice McLachlin describe the rule as". At times, it may be useful to add the initial of the first name of a judge when there are two or three judges with the same surname. One no longer uses the locution, "As he then was". It follows that one eliminates the adjective "learned" in front of the names of the counsel who pled. Simply say, "Counsel for the plaintiff submitted that . . . ".

Here is another interesting example found in the opinion of Cory J. in *R.* v. *Edwards*[22]. Although long, it is easy to follow because it is developed logically:

> A review of the recent decisions of this Court and those of the U.S. Supreme Court, which I find convincing and properly applicable to the situation presented in the case at bar, indicates that certain principles pertaining to the nature of the s. 8 right to be secure against unreasonable search or seizure can be derived. In my view, they may be summarized in the following manner:
>
> 1. A claim for relief under s. 24(2) can only be made by the person whose *Charter* rights have been infringed. See *R. v. Rahey*, [1987] 1 S.C.R. 588, at p. 619.
>
> 2. Like all *Charter* rights, s. 8 is a personal right. It protects people and not places. See *Hunter, supra.*
>
> 3. The right to challenge the legality of a search depends upon the accused establishing that his personal rights to privacy have been violated. See *Pugliese, supra.*

---

22. [1996] 1 S.C.R. 128, 146.

4. As a general rule, two distinct inquiries must be made in relation to s. 8. First, has the accused a reasonable expectation of privacy. Second, if he has such an expectation, was the search by the police conducted reasonably. See *Rawlings, supra.*

5. A reasonable expectation of privacy is to be determined on the basis of the totality of the circumstances. See *Colarusso, supra,* at p. 54, and *Wong, supra,* at p. 62.

6. The factors to be considered in assessing the totality of the circumstances may include, but are not restricted to, the following:

   (i) presence at the time of the search;

   (ii) possession or control of the property or place searched;

   (iii) ownership of the property or place;

   (iv) historical use of the property or item;

   (v) the ability to regulate access, including the right to admit or exclude others from the place;

   (vi) the existence of a subjective expectation of privacy; and

   (vii) the objective reasonableness of the expectation.

   See *United States v. Gomez,* 16 F.3d 254 (8th Cir. 1994), at p. 256.

7. If an accused person establishes a reasonable expectation of privacy, the inquiry must proceed to the second stage to determine whether the search was conducted in a reasonable manner.

The list of authorities

Traditionally, in complicated matters where questions of law are debated, judges add to the end of the judgment a list of authorities cited by counsel and consulted by whoever pronounced the judgment.

Is this useful, and, if yes, to whom? Having regard to the time required to put the list together, the question is worth thinking about. Although accessory, such a list may prove useful despite the fact that law reports normally do not reproduce them. Firstly, they are useful as a guide for future research on a given subject. Since you easily remember having rendered a decision on a certain subject, the list can serve as an inventory of the jurisprudence on the subject. This can be of help to your colleagues and to lawyers, law students and law professors.

Additionally, the list will give an indication to courts of appeal if a particular authority was brought to the attention of the court of first instance. At times, the argument before a court of appeal centres principally on whether a particular decision of the Supreme Court was the subject of discussion before the trial judge. This is particularly so in common law jurisdictions where precedent is important.

Since counsel frequently prepare these lists as support for their arguments, it is a simple matter to annex them to the judgment.

Nevertheless, it is better to list only the leading authorities on a subject. If there are several, group them under headings. Above all, don't lose sight of the objective of conciseness.

Where to put the citation?

Law review articles, monograms and doctoral theses cite the source of quoted passages at the end of a chapter or of the work. Not surprisingly, this is the preference of editors. However, a decision responds to different imperatives: to repeat, a decision is an act of communication. To help this communication, the source should be immediately available and be placed at the bottom of the page of the quote or in the body of the text, immediately after having identified the parties.

The insertion of these reference notes and page notes, whether referring to a reported case, a textbook, an article, follow strict conventions. A good reference tool is *Canadian Guide to Uniform Legal Citation*[23].

When one refers to a case or a textbook, the name of the parties or the title of the work must be emphasized with underlining, capital letters, bold or italics.

Illustration:

- In the matter of *Tremblay* v. *Daigle* [1989] 2 S.C.R. 530, the Supreme Court of Canada decided that . . ..
- Peter McWilliams, in the 4th edition of his work *Canadian Criminal Evidence* defines clearly the . . ..

Note: When an author is well-known in legal circles, mention of his first and last names is sufficient. This avoids the difficulty following any change of position or office by the author after the publication of a work and its subsequent editions.

Avoid at all costs imprecise reference to jurisprudence of the sort: "The jurisprudence is consistent in this regard", without mentioning at least one case, unless you are referring to a fundamental rule such as that which obliges a judge to hear the other side before making a decision. If the principle is obvious, just set it out.

Do not write: The text writers and the cases establish that there must be a causal connection between a negligent act and the injury sustained for a plaintiff to recover.

Instead, put the sentence in an affirmative tone: "There must be a causal connection between ..., etc."

Additional illustration:

American jurisprudence similarly refuses to order the payment of an indemnity in the name of damages, in the absence of proof

23. 1992 Trustees of the McGill Law Journal Trust Fund, 3rd Ed., Carswell.

of actual prejudice. In addition, it is a condition of payment of an indemnity that the claimants prove bad faith on the part of the employer: *Publishers' Association of New York City (New York Times and New York Printing Pressmen's Union No. 2: (37 LA 509, pp. 519-520).*

* * * * *

Illustration: (to be avoided)

[Translation]

I remember having read somewhere about a prostitute having been brought before the courts for having omitted to pay her income tax. She maintained that the profession which she practised was illegal, forbidden by law, that in consequence she didn't have to pay taxes to the government; she maintained that the government could not tax illegality. I forget if this matter was pleaded here, in Canada, or in the United States, but, in any event, I remember that this prostitute was ordered to pay taxes on the annual revenue ascribed to her by the tax collectors. I was, and I remain, perfectly in agreement with that decision and I remain convinced that, if the same case, appeared in front of our courts, the prostitute would be ordered to pay the tax on that income established as earned by her.

I give this example simply to explain my view of these things. It is true that article 5 of the law stipulates that the Minister must refuse a registration certificate to someone who does not obey the laws of the Liquor Control Board. This power of the Minister exists with the goal of assuring the more effective control on sales made by tavern owners; nevertheless, it doesn't deprive the Minister to claim taxes for illegal sales of alcoholic beverages.

The method which follows is surely more satisfying and effective:

Keane J. – In general, bodies which are not courts but which exercise functions of a judicial or quasi-judicial nature determining legal rights and obligations must give reasons for their decisions, because of the requirements of constitutional and natural justice and in order to ensure that the superior courts may exercise their jurisdiction to enquire into and, if necessary, correct such decisions: see *The State (Creedon) v. The Criminal Injuries Compensation Tribunal* [1988] I.R. 51. The requirement to give reasons may extend even further to purely administrative bodies, at least where their decisions affect legal rights and obligations: see *International Fishing Vessels Ltd. v. The Minister for the Marine*, [1989] I.R. 149.

* * * * *

4. Do not be prolix

Words are like leaves; and where they most abound,
Much fruit of sense beneath is rarely found.

Alexander Pope

It is hard to resist the temptation to describe one's doubts or to describe the pangs of giving birth to a decision.

Some feel the need to express at what point the decision was difficult, or at what price of intellectual efforts their masterpiece was born. Futile. Others feel bound to say that they have dutifully carried out their responsibilities. Write these thoughts in your draft if it helps, but remove them from the final text.

The judgment alone as rendered should bear witness to the work accomplished. The work is not measured according to the number of written pages, quite the reverse. To write less takes more time.

Moreover, everyone assumes that people charged with the responsibility of rendering justice do so with all the competence they have. To say so in the judgment is redundant.

Illustrations: Some texts gleaned from the Law Reports:

1- "I wish to make it clear that I have gone through the entire list of cases submitted to me by Mr. X for the claimant, some 20 in all, which are the leading cases in this field. I have also reviewed the 30 cases cited to me by Mr. Z on this issue, many, of course, overlapping with those cited by plaintiff's counsel."

2- "After some reflexion, it would seem to me that the latter interpretation is the correct one..."

3- "There is no doubt that there are formidable arguments to be made on both sides of this vexing question."

4- "I have reviewed the whole of the evidence and submissions and referred to the evidence extensively."

5- "In the result of the foregoing as I understood it, he considered that [...]"

"Reverting for a moment to the evidence of Mr. X it should, I think, be noted that he agreed that [...] in the result, as I understood his evidence, he agreed that..."

6- "On all the evidence before me, weighed with scrupulous care, I find that..."

7- "The facts relating to this matter, although important, are essentially not the issue. It is the application of the law to the facts and circumstances that gives rise to some difficulty and caused me to reserve my decision at the close of the trial, to permit me to review the evidence, but more particularly, to review the authorities presented in argument by both counsel for the accused and the Crown. I should point out that the accused was not in custody and will not be unduly inconvenienced by my decision to reserve to consider my verdict."

8- "The court believes itself judicially justified."

9- "The court has no hesitation, in this case, to apply section XYZ of the Act."

10- "On the application here of the principles contained in the words that I have quoted, the opinion seems unavoidable, although I must confess that the acceptance of it is not entirely to my liking, that the defendant must be held liable for the consequences suffered by the plaintiff as a result of the defendant's logging activities carried on above the plaintiff's right-of-way. Here, it is not a question of the defendant having failed to take any positive steps to ensure that the run-off did not injure the plaintiff, which, of course, it does not have to do. The situation that prevails here, in my view, is that by positive steps the defendant caused the surface water to run from its land in such a manner as to change materially the velocity and direction of its flow and thus to cause injury to the plaintiff by the washout of its pipeline. In addition, in my view of the evidence, the defendant was negligent in that after having created the situation that caused the material changes to which I have just referred, it then failed to take the comparatively simple steps that would have avoided the unfortunate consequences of the situation it had created. Accordingly, it seems to me that the claim can properly be maintained in nuisance."

11- "While I hold without hesitation, as I now do, that the plaintiff bank took the defendant's notes without consideration, I necessarily do so without entire confidence that my opinion will accord with future decisions of higher courts, eminent authority having pronounced the question, upon which I am compelled to decide, a difficult one, and on that account having refrained from expressing an opinion upon it."

To end this matter, imagine the losing party's dissatisfaction on receipt of the following opinion, delivered by a judge in 1897 – succinct it must be said, but somewhat less than forthright: [translation]

Taschereau J. – I have experienced considerable difficulty in coming to a conclusion in this case, and I am far from sure that the appellant should succeed. However, it would be useless for me to hold up the judgment or to enter a dissent. I concur, *dubitante*.

* * * * *

CHAPTER V

REVISION

There is no such thing as good writing,
there is only good rewriting.

Louis D. Brandeis

Written language can give a more faithful image of thought because it can be revised. To write is to rewrite.

We cannot stress too strongly the importance of revision of the text of a decision before its communication to the parties.

Several plans, several drafts, several revisions: that is the necessary process in constructing a judgment.

A word processor can make this task much easier. However, a danger lurks: the temptation to correct time and again at the cost of intolerable delay. A judgment rendered promptly, even if stylistically imperfect, is worth more than a judgment whose style is impeccable, but whose arrival is long overdue.

As in all things, strive for a happy medium.

To carry out a proper revision, it is necessary to draw back from the text awhile, becoming, in a way, a stranger to it. To this end, set it aside for a period; a day or two if possible. The hoped-for distancing should readily follow. If time presses, ask someone to read the text, a colleague perhaps.

Here is what John Kenneth Galbraith[24] had to say about revision:

---

24. *Writing, Typing, and Economics,* Atlantic Monthly, March 1978.

> To write adequately one must know, above all, how bad are one's first drafts. They are bad because the need to combine composition with thought, both in their own way taxing, leads initially to a questionable, even execrable, result. With each revision the task eases, the product improves. Eventually there could be clarity and perhaps even grace. Anthony Trollope tells proudly in his autobiography that he never sent a manuscript to his publisher without reading it over at least once with care. My commitment is to no fewer than five revisions; this I trust, sprightly document, has had six.

Why revise? In four words: to polish the style. In several words:

1. **To remove superfluous details and useless repetition.**

2. **To remove superfluous emphasis.**

Illustrations:

(1) The witness lied *considerably*.

(2) The plaintiff, on the other hand, is an honest person and *very* frank.

(3) He demonstrated *great* wickedness.

(4) The matter is *excessively* difficult for the court to resolve.

(5) The court is *very* conscious that in thus finding ...

(6) The court after having *carefully* consulted section 23 of the Act ...

3. **To eliminate pleonasms, clichés, verbiage, redundant expressions, grammatical errors.**

A pleonasm is the repetition of two terms which have the same meaning. This repetition can operate to give more force to an idea, but if it adds nothing it should be eliminated.

Illustrations:

Pleonasm: Predict in advance, add together, compare between them, at this point in time, etc.

Clichés: "With deference to those who think otherwise".

"The learned trial judge".

"I am constrained to conclude."

Verbiage: "If I am not mistaken and if I have truly understood the gist of the authorities".

"At the trial I was under the impression that under these circumstances the state of the law – contrary to what I thought it ought to be – would not permit of my holding otherwise than that the plaintiffs became holders of the notes for valuable consideration without notice of defect in the company's title to the notes, and had I remained of this impression I would have given judgment for the plaintiffs, with a stay, however, of execution for six months, with a view that by that time either the plaintiffs, who, besides other collateral security, hold the guarantee bond of the individual directors, would have collected the whole balance owing them, and thus would not be entitled to enforce the judgment; or the defendant, if so advised, might take proceedings against the individual directors for indemnity. Having reserved judgment, and had an opportunity of looking into the authorities, I now give judgment for the defendant with costs, [...]".

4. **To find substitutes for the verbs: to be, to have, to make, and to the expressions "there are"; "to the effect that", etc.**

5. **To tighten the text, to render it more concise and to verify the precision of words and abbreviations.**

Illustration:

– A cheque in the amount of $3,500.00	– A cheque for $3,500.
– The written letter dated May 7, 1994 to quit the premises.	– The notice to quit dated May 7, 1994.

Eliminate the compound prepositions:

– In favour of	– For
– For the reason that	– Because
– In the event that	– If
– Subsequent to	– After
– Prior to	– Before

One readily accepts certain abbreviations: v. (versus), c. or chap. (chapter), ff. (following), p.(page). Everything depends on the context. If there is any possibility of confusion, write the word in full.

6. **To avoid sexist expressions and turns of phrase.**

Everyone writing for the public today should be aware of the importance of avoiding sexist language. In editorial rooms, in legislative offices, in the communication sector, gender neutral language is a constant preoccupation – and rightly so.

It is not enough to say that the use of sexist language is unconscious, or that its exclusion of women is unintentional. Words such as "craftsman", "mankind", "businessman", and "policeman" are potentially offensive to many people of both sexes, particularly when ready substitutes are available – "artisan", "humanity", "business person", and "police officer".

Common pitfalls include: the use of "man" as a collective for both sexes; job titles which exclude women such as "postman"; using the masculine singular personal pronoun "his" or "him" when using the plural "their" and "them" avoids the problem; treating wives as adjuncts to husbands; automatically describing women as "charming" or "attractive".

An essential part of revision is to identify lapses as described above and correct them with appropriate alternatives. The learning in this area is vast; the bibliography which follows the text includes only a sampling of the help available.

Some recommended alternatives outrage grammatical purists, while others may, admittedly, strain a rule – "Everyone brought their book" can fall gratingly on some ears; the repeated use of "his or her" can be stylistically awkward at times. Nevertheless, which is preferable? To transgress against grammar and felicity, or to risk offending or ignoring a significant part of humanity? For judges and those ever conscious of equality rights, we say the answer is clear.

7. **To verify the punctuation.**

In revising, one will verify the punctuation. The principle function of punctuation is to ensure clarity of the sentence. It gives rhythm to the text and permits the reader to take a breath. Writing breathes by its commas.

In the case of legal language, punctuation plays an important role. Construction of statutes by the courts depends upon it. In the drafting of judgments one ought to pay particular attention to punctuation. A simple comma or an apostrophe can completely change the sense of a judgment or of a phrase:

The butler called the guests' names as they entered.

The butler called the guests names as they entered.

How many revisions are necessary?

Several. Some writers do as many as seven or eight. At least three are required to produce a text sufficiently polished.

Here is an example of four steps of revision:

1- 29th October 1976. – The plaintiff Gilbert Watmough alleges that he entered into an agreement to purchase a D6 caterpillar tractor from the defendant, Cap's Construction ltd., and that the defendant wrongfully refused to deliver the D6 to him. The plaintiff alleges that the agreement was reduced to writing by him and that he signed as purchaser and that John Capostinsky signed as an officer of the defendant company, the vendor. The said agreement is Ex. 1. The plaintiff further alleges that the agreement was signed on 23rd May 1975, sometime before 10:30 a.m., and that after a brief time, approximately 1½ hours, during which he located a trucker who was to remove the D6 caterpillar, John Capostinsky refused to permit the plaintiff to take the D6 caterpillar. Capostinsky subsequently returned the cheques that the plaintiff had handed to him on 23rd May 1975.

2- Gilbert Watmough agreed to purchase a D6 caterpillar tractor from the defendant, who wrongfully refused to deliver it to him. The agreement was signed on the 23rd May 1975, sometime before 10:30 a.m., by G. Watmough as the purchaser and by John Capostinsky, as an officer of the vendor.

Approximately 1½ hours later, during which Watmough located a trucker to remove the D6 caterpillar, Capostinsky refused to permit the removal of the D6. Capostinsky subsequently returned the cheques that Watmough had handed to him on 23rd May 1975.

3- Gilbert Watmough signed with John Capostinsky, as an officer of the vendor, on May 23rd, 1975, sometime before 10:30 a.m., an agreement to purchase a D6 caterpillar tractor.

Approximately $1\frac{1}{2}$ hours later, during which Watmough located a trucker to remove the tractor, Capostinsky refused to permit its removal. Capostinsky subsequently returned the cheques that Watmough had handed to him on May 23rd, 1975.

4- Sometime before 10:30 a.m. on May 23, 1975, Gilbert Watmough and John Capostinsky, an officer of the defendant, signed an agreement for the purchase of a D6 caterpillar tractor.

During the $1\frac{1}{2}$ hours that followed, Watmough found a trucker to remove the tractor, but Capostinsky refused to permit its removal. Capostinsky then returned the cheques Watmough had handed to him on signing.

Evidently, a judgment is not a novel, and judges don't have the luxury to put a draft aside for two months or so. Imperatives of justice require a certain speed. However, it is often possible to place the first draft of a judgment in a drawer for 48 hours before revising it. Letting it lie fallow gives enough distancing to make the necessary corrections.

CHAPTER VI

THE ORAL JUDGMENT

Must every judge's decision be written? Certainly not. Every day, in Canada and elsewhere, judges give countless oral decisions. They include rulings given during the course of a trial, interlocutory motions, and judgments at the conclusion of the trial.

An obvious advantage of an oral judgment is one less matter reserved. This can only improve the judge's calendar and frame of mind. The second benefit is the removal of temptation to recodify the law and write a judgment more suitable for a learned article than a decision at the conclusion of a trial; trial judges should make adequate findings of fact and apply the law as they understand it. If wrong in law, courts of appeal can correct the decision without the necessity of ordering a new trial.

A third virtue of an oral judgment is its effect on the parties to the litigation. Having undergone some years of stress awaiting the outcome, they have their trial – they get their result. Surely the losing party is less likely to appeal than where the result appears weeks or months later.

Five special considerations apply to oral judgments:

1. Under no circumstances can they be extemporaneous or unstructured.

2. The principles of good judgment writing apply equally to oral judgments.

3. Backsliding from the principles of judgment writing is depressingly easy when giving an oral judgment.

4. Oral judgments attract the use of euphemisms.

5. Oral judgments induce excessive judicial modesty.

1. The extemporaneous or unstructured oral judgment

Consider the following:

> "Ah – yes – I follow that – but I am not sure where it takes us – I, er [inaudible] the point could be, that, but [unintelligible] but it could be otherwise. It could be so in some other case because the key here is the issue of well, identity, I don't really mean identity, I mean reliability, I mean credibility. I mean, you know, has the Crown done it or not? The golden thread sort of stuff – I thought that after Mr. Grey was finished they hadn't done it but they have. Everything is here – rather there, and I don't have much – I mean any hesitation in concluding notwithstanding the able points made by Mr. White – I mean Grey – so eloquently that you are, after all is said and done, with everything being considered, you are guilty."

To receive something along this line from a court reporter is a sobering experience. The reminder is clear – writing is not speech written down writing is revision; speech, once delivered, cannot be revised.

An oral judgment is, by definition, a "reserved oral judgment". It may be fifteen minutes, it may be the noon recess, it may be overnight, it may even be a week or more, but implicit in the concept of an oral judgment is a period of time taken to establish the issues to be decided, to make findings of fact and law, and to come to a conclusion – all drafted in block or point form. Having created the first draft, now is the time to revise. Unbelievable as it may seem, the earlier example can be considered a first draft – not a good one perhaps, but capable of revision into something useful.

2. The principles of good judgment writing apply equally to oral judgments

(a) Having made available the time necessary for revision, use it to apply the principles discussed in preceding chapters. Just as a good written judgment is reader based, so a good oral judgment is listener based. Who are the most important persons in the courtroom on the day the judgment is delivered? Surely they are the parties – particularly the losing party. The judgment should show why the suit was lost and how the judge arrived at the result.

(b) Identify the issues whether of fact or law. In cases where argument is not recorded, place on the record any agreements as to facts not in issue or the point of law to be determined, if such agreements exist.

(c) Avoid the use of jargon or legalese. They have even less place in an oral judgment than a written one. As discussed below, this is easier said than done.

(d) Whether you state the result at the outset or at the conclusion is a matter of personal choice. One thing is sure, decide the result before starting the judgment. Spare the litigants a voyage of discovery, stopping here and there, retracing your steps, and indulging in side trips. To quote the Honourable William Stevenson, formerly of the Supreme Court of Canada "That voyage of discovery is one you should take on your own so that when you do it for pay in front of an audience, you do it efficiently and effectively. We are professional communicators and should do the job professionally."

(e) In the course of preparing oral judgments, every judge will no doubt work towards a personal model. Without attempting to prescribe a particular method, it is fair to note those features that should be in every model including:

(i) The identification of parties and the cause – who did what to whom, and what are the issues to be decided?

(ii) A review of the facts required to support the findings.

(iii) Findings of fact.

(iv) Statement of the controlling law and its application to the facts as found.

(v) A conclusion responsive to the relief claimed, incorporated in a judgment.

3. Back sliding

Unfortunately, it is far too easy to slide away from the principles of judgment writing when delivering an oral decision. The temptation is to rely upon familiar expressions while thinking of what to say next. All too often, these false friends spring from jargon and legalese. Givers of oral judgments have an abhorrence of "dead air" – they believe if they stop and think for 30 seconds before continuing, somehow those in the courtroom will think less of their ability. Yet the record will never show the pause for thought, nor its length. Rather than lard the transcript with jargon and legalese, take the time to think of what next to say, and say it in plain, clear language.

4. The temptation of euphemism

Euphemism is the substitution of an inoffensive word for one considered offensively explicit. This causes judges to say a witness "has a nodding acquaintance with the truth", or "has been less than candid with the court." Other examples include referring to a lower court judge as the "learned trial judge" when what follows is a finding that establishes the judge is anything but. If a witness has tried to deceive the court, say so. Despite the presence of an accused about to be convicted, or a party about to lose the litigation, judges should avoid diluting the force of their findings by trying to be all things to all people. They must recognize that almost invariably, someone will leave the courtroom highly displeased with the result. However, unambiguous findings will help persuade the losing party to at least accept the result if not agree with it.

5. The perils of judicial modesty

In the presence of the parties, judges are tempted to soften the blow for the losing party by comments designed to show how complex the matter was, how close it was to going the other way, and the struggle undergone to arrive at the result. Of course, humility, courtesy, sympathy, and anxious concern are human emotions which every judge should exhibit in full measure. However, translated into uncertainty, they impair persuasiveness. No-one, least of all John McEnroe, would be impressed by an umpire saying, "Oh well, with difficulty, I am of the view, with deference to those who think otherwise, that, on balance, well, it's out."

By way of illustration, consider the decision of a sensitive and compassionate judge who, perhaps, disclosed too much of his thought processes. During his reason for convicting an accused of sexual assault he found:

> I found D to be right, articulate, and honest. Despite some contradictions and inconsistencies, her testimony was generally reliable and internally coherent on key details. While I am acutely aware of the dangers of convicting on the evidence of a young child, I found that her testimony had the ring of truth. ... In addition, her straightforward and non-vindictive manner and ready intelligent response in the witness box reinforced the impression of frankness. ... Suffice to say that despite a few discrepancies in her testimony, I believed D's story. ...
>
> I find the evidence of the accused and his wife unreliable and self serving. The accused's explanation for his presence on the two occasions was both threadbare and unpersuasive. Moreover, his testimony unfolded smoothly, it did not ring true. ... Regrettably, I attach little weight to his testimony.

However, the judge went on to say:

> In several ways this is a tragic case involving trauma to a child of tender years and the prospect of permanent alienation between members of the same family. Because the Court is human and fallible, it does not have the unerring eye of God. It must, therefore, seek to achieve justice on the basis of evidence and rules of law. Proof beyond a reasonable doubt does not connote absolute certainty, but rather that degree of proof which convinces the mind and satisfied the conscience. Such a degree of proof exists here, and I feel compelled to act upon it.

The Court of Appeal ordered a new trial:

> We would not and could not interfere with the learned trial judge's determination of credibility, were it not for the tenor of the reasons for judgment which disclose an error of law in his appreciation of the evidence.

An additional half-hour revision before delivery may have helped avoid a retrial.

CHAPTER VII

STYLE

Proper words in proper places.

Jonathan Swift

Each field of knowledge has its own style, its own exclusive vocabulary. The severe criticisms aimed at juridical jargon abound because the language of jurists is ancient, responds to imperatives of stability and uniformity, and labours under its own linguistic restraints. It is a specialized language.

Professor Raymond describes what is necessary jargon and what is not25:

> Some kinds of pretentious diction are called "jargon". Jargon is a special language of a particular field or profession. Jargon has its legitimate uses. We cannot expect lawyers to say *habeas corpus* in English, or football players to find a synonym for a "post pattern", or psychologists to avoid "sociopathic", or musicians to abandon "*andante cantabile*" just because the rest of us may not understand these terms. The jargon of any given field is often the most efficient means of communication within that field.
>
> Jargon becomes offensive, however, when there are handy English equivalents available or when people outside the field are expected to understand what is said. [...]

The style of a decision will reflect the usages established in each jurisdiction of various countries and legal systems. Style will also vary according to the personality of the writer, as seen in some examples below.

However, every judicial style should be governed by two guiding principles. First, style must not exclude or offend the

25. *Writing (Is an Unnatural Act), op. cit.*, p. 144.

litigants or the wider audience; rather it must show how the law is applied to particular facts, while demonstrating respect to the parties and the impartiality of the writer, all expressed in clear, accessible language. Second, a judgment is not a chance to voice personal views, no matter how entertainingly expressed; rather, it should serve the parties by identifying the issues and rendering a decision.

A. Comparison of judgment writing styles in France, Britain and the United States

In 1976, an article entitled *Characteristics of Judicial Style in France, Britain, and the USA* appeared in The American Journal of Comparative Law. Written by Professor Jean-Louis Goutal, the article described the principal characteristics of judgment writing in each country.

In France, since the time of the Revolution, the courts used nothing other than deductive reasoning. At the highest level, the Cour de Cassation favours syllogism, short and simple. Although French courts of appeal set out the facts at greater length, the structure of their judgments is identical: they work deductively from a premise which enunciates a general principle.

In Britain, just the opposite happens, writes Professor Goutal. Decisions generally begin with a long recital of the facts, sometimes in the form of a story, often followed by inductive reasoning using a comparative method, eliminating in passing the various possible solutions until but one remains. In this process, recourse is made to precedents that are scrutinized and used where applicable. Professor Goutal compares the two systems thus:

> [...] This distinction is crucial: the French opinion, in which reasoning starts at the first line, is nothing but a pure form of reasoning, whereas the English opinion, in which reasoning appears only after a lengthy introduction is a discursive process, incidentally integrating various forms of reasoning.

The professor's analysis emphasises the difference in the length of the judgments, those from France proving significantly shorter.

As for the American style of judgment writing, Professor Goutal describes it in these terms:

> For induction is inseparable from a high level of individualization. It requires tremendous work on the facts and the circumstances, unknown to a judge devoted to deduction, like the French Cour de Cassation. Individualization (assuming it had been otherwise favoured by the members of the court system) became impossible with the growing case load. At the turn of the 19th century, any state supreme court would handle several hundred cases per year, whereas the case load of the House of Lords had never exceeded, and still is today, about 50 cases per year.
>
> This state of affairs necessitated standardization. But there could be no standardization without systematization, which in turn entailed abstraction.
>
> [...]
>
> This shift to deduction and the trend to abstraction are a crucial part of the general transformation of the process of adjudication in America in the 19th century. [...] This shift reflects, in our view, the most impressive characteristic of the American legal system: beyond systemization, abstraction signifies a surprising marriage of Common Law and Civil Law traditions. That marriage occurred because both cultures co-existed in the land, and because the union was wanted.
>
> They co-existed: on one side, the dominant Common Law background – dominant mainly in that the law was administered by people with a Common Law education and mentality rather than because the law stuff itself was Common Law. On the other side, many areas had an 'indigenous' Civil Law background; some French, some Spanish.

* * * * *

B. In Canada

In Canada, two legal regimes co-exist and are in full bloom: the common law and the civil law have developed in parallel and have at times cross-fertilized. Justice Charles Gonthier, at the August 1997 Canadian Bar Annual Conference reflected that "in fact, in spite of the apparent divergence in their approach to legal sources, the common law and the civil law currently reap the benefits of their reciprocal influence".

The two systems can be seen in the legislative drafting styles when comparing the Civil Code of Quebec and a common law statute like the Copyright Act or the Competition Act[26], for example. And of course, these drafting styles influence the drafting of judgments or decisions.

Sandra C. Markman, writing on legislative bijuralism[27] identifies four potential groups of readers of federal legislation: civil law Anglophones, civil law Francophones, common law Anglophones and common law Francophones. She illustrates some of the bijuralism problems and possible solutions when drafting legislation:

> There are various techniques that may be used to solve the problems of legislative bijuralism. As is always the case in drafting, the virtue of brevity is in conflict with that of completeness. The tension is generally between finding a drafting technique for a provision that uses terminology easily recognizable by the members of each of the four audiences and drafting in a way that is not overly long and complex. The plain language advocates tell us there is no reason to use the lawyers' standby "null and void" but the drafter mindful of the sensibilities of the two English-speaking audiences will want "null" for civil lawyers and "void" for common lawyers. As is the case for so many things, drafters and the departments for which they draft make choices on a case-by-case basis.

26. S.C. c. C-42 and C-34.
27. Senior Counsel, Department of Justice, Canada, at the Canadian Bar Annual Meeting, August 1997.

In writing a decision however, a judge will try to identify its audience and to choose the appropriate language. While legislative drafters need to canvass the widest audiences in Canada, the drafters of decisions are usually working in a narrower setting, since the legal regime is either the common law or the civil law, save in those rare cases where both systems apply.

C. Some examples of judicial styles

There can be as many judicial styles as there are judges. Nonetheless, at least four broad categories can be identified which include 95% of judgments written – called, for our purposes, the imperial, the literary, the methodical, and the colloquial.

The Imperial Style

The imperial style resonates with the echoing thunder of the Old Testament. Popular before the Second World War, it is less so nowadays, reserved for weighty issues of universal importance. When put to proper use, it can be powerfully persuasive. Here is Justice Oliver Wendell Holmes on freedom of expression:

> When men have realized that time has upset many fighting faiths, they may come to believe ... that the ultimate good desired is better reached by free trade in ideas – that the best test of truth is the power of thought to get itself accepted in the competition of the market. ... We should be eternally vigilant against attempts to check the expression of opinions that we loathe and believe to be fraught with death, unless they so imminently threaten immediate interference with the lawful and pressing purposes of the law, that an immediate check is required to save the country.

For an example of a judge carried away with this style, contrast the dissenting opinion in *United States v. Ulysses*[28], which novel Judge Manton found to be obscene:

28. 72 F. 2d 705 (1934).

> Congress passed this statute against obscenity for the protection of the great mass of our people; the unusual literator can, or thinks he can, protect himself. The people do not exist for the sake of literature, to give the author fame, the publisher wealth, and the book a market. On the contrary, literature exists for the sake of the people, to refresh the weary, to console the sad, to hearten the dull and downcast, to increase man's interest in the world, his joy of living, and his sympathy in all sorts of conditions of men. Art for art's sake is heartless and soon grows artless; art for the public market is not art at all, but commerce; art for the people's service is a noble, vital, and permanent element of human life.
>
> The public is content with the standard of saleability; the prigs with the standard of preciosity. The people need and deserve a moral standard; it should be a point of honour with men of letters to maintain it. Masterpieces have never been produced by men given to obscenity or lustful thoughts – men who have no Master. Reverence for good work is the foundation of literary character. A refusal to imitate obscenity or to load a book with it is an author's professional chastity.
>
> Good work in literature has its permanent mark; it is like all good work, noble and lasting. It requires a human aim – to cheer, console, purify, or ennoble the life of people. Without this aim, literature has never sent an arrow close to the mark. It is by good work only that men of letters can justify their right to a place in the world.

Subsequently, Judge Manton was carried away in another sense – he was convicted of accepting bribes for revealing his judgments prior to issue.

The Literary Style

This style, while less grandiloquent than the imperial, retains many of the latter's characteristics. Latinate words abound, rhetorical devices flourish. Although seen more often now than the Imperial style, its use overall has diminished in the last 15 years.

As an example of its effective use, here is Justice Felix Frankfurter[29] in the course of withdrawing from a case because of his strong feeling about the issue:

> The judicial process demands that a judge move within the framework of relevant legal rules and the covenanted modes of thought for ascertaining them. He must think dispassionately and submerge private feeling on every aspect of a case. There is a good deal of shallow talk that the judicial robe does not change the man within it. It does. The fact is that on the whole judges do lay aside private views in discharging their judicial functions. This is achieved through training, professional habits, self-discipline and that fortunate alchemy by which men are loyal to the obligation with which they are entrusted. But it is also true that reason cannot control the subconscious influence of feelings of which it is unaware. When there is ground for believing that such unconscious feelings may operate in the ultimate judgment, or may not unfairly lead others to believe they are operating, judges recuse themselves. They do not sit in judgment. They do this for a variety of reasons. The guiding consideration is that the administration of justice should reasonably appear to be disinterested as well as be so in fact.

Contrast the above with this turgid example of the literary style:

> The allegations in the complaint, taken at their face value, show notice to the parents of the dangerous propensities of their minor son, an inability to control him in that regard and a complete default in restraining him from conduct calculated to harm others which by reason of his prior antics could reasonably have been anticipated. The parents therefore owed a duty to society to guard their son closely to see to it that he did not indulge in his vicious propensities.

The Methodical Style

The methodical style appeals to judges for whom deductive reasoning is the key to finding the correct result. This style lends itself to headings, sub-headings and points (a), (b), and

29. 343 U.S. 451 (1952).

(c), moving inexorably from one to the next. Usually the language is neutral, plain and observes the rhythms of ordinary speech – it can be flat and uninteresting in unskillful practitioners. Here is Justice Peter Cory skillfully using the methodical style while considering whether a threat of rape was a threat to cause serious bodily harm:

> For the purposes of s. 264.1(1)(a) of the **Criminal Code** "serious bodily harm" means any hurt or injury, whether physical or psychological, that interferes in a substantial way with the integrity, health or well-being of a victim. To determine whether spoken or written words constitute a threat to cause serious bodily harm they must be looked at in the context in which they were spoken or written, in light of the person to whom they were addressed and the circumstances in which they were uttered. They should be viewed in an objective way and the meaning attributed to the words should be that which a reasonable person would give to them. A threat of rape in and of itself considered in light of the context of the written words or conversation in which the threat was made and of the person to whom the words were addressed may constitute a threat to cause serious bodily harm. In this case the threats contained in the letters constitute a threat to cause serious bodily harm.

The Colloquial Style

This style is characterized by plain language, colloquialisms, and is not above the odd slang expression. The emphasis is on clarity and accessibility; when overdone it can create a tone of informality which some may find inappropriate in a judgment.

In a model of clarity and accessibility, a Newfoundland judge dealt with an itinerant piece of glass:

> **O'Regan J.** – Annie Carew and two friends went to Midway Gardens one evening for a pizza. Annie bit into a piece of glass she claims was in the pizza. She thought she swallowed some of the glass so she called the hospital and followed their advise. The next day she attended for x-rays which were inconclusive. However, some days later she experienced

> slight bleeding from her bowel and found minute glass particles in her stool. She now sues for damages.
>
> The Defendant company denies liability because they claim their method of food preparation is so careful that the glass couldn't get into their pizza. The Defendant explained their preparation and I agree that they take great care in preparing their food. The owner of the company also admitted that glasses do break in the restaurant but they take great care to clean up. It is clear that glass when broken travels well! It is for this reason that the Plaintiff pleads Res Ipsa Loquitur. In such a claim against a manufacturer the Plaintiff should only fail when on the mass of evidence the Court is left in doubt as to whether or not negligence ought to be inferred ... .
>
> I am not saying that the Defendant company runs a loose operation. On the contrary the Defendant enjoys a well deserved reputation in the community. Even the Plaintiff who also works in the food industry still recommends the Defendant's pizzas. However, even with its good reputation the Defendant owes a duty of care to its customers and in this case must be liable for its actions.

The following example is not so successful:

> To interpret the Act, admittedly passed for the benefit of wives, in any other way would make the Act in many cases one to a wife's detriment. Can it be said, as against the wife of a man who has progressed in life from humble beginnings and whose first married home was a mere "but and ben" and whose last residence was a stately mansion, that, because the wife had not consented in writing to the change of residence, her life estate is only in the two-roomed shack and not in the new "homestead"? I think not. The purpose of the section is to prevent the husband without the wife's consent changing the residence to her detriment.

Of course, there are those styles which defy classification because of their individuality. No one better exemplifies this category than Lord Denning. Space dictates only three of many examples:

New Windsor Corp. v. Mellor

Today we look back far in time to a town or village green. The turf is old. Animals have grazed there for hundreds of years. Nowadays they are pleasant stretches of grass where people sit and talk. Sometimes they play cricket or kick a ball about. But in medieval times it was the place where the young men mustered with their bows and arrows. They shot at the butts. There might be stocks there where offenders were put for their petty misdemeanours. In the month of May they set up a maypole and danced around it. We have no record of when it all began, but the poet tells us:

> "On the green they watched their sons
> Playing till too dark to see,
> As their fathers watched them once,
> As my father once watched me . . ."

Bremer Vulkan v. South India Shipping

When I was young, a sandwich-man wearing a top-hat used to parade outside these courts with his boards back and front, proclaiming `Arbitrate don't litigate'. It was very good advice so long as arbitrations were conducted speedily: as many, still are in the City of London. But it is not so good when arbitrations drag on for ever.

Rank Film v. Video Centre

"It is, it is a glorious thing, to be a Pirate King," said W.S. Gilbert (The Pirates of Penzance, I). But he was speaking of ship pirates. Today we speak of film pirates. It is not a glorious thing to be, but it is a good thing to be in for making money.

Of course, not everyone can write like Lord Denning, nor should anyone try. However, everyone has an individual voice, and with a little effort (can let it?) grace their decisions. Take, for example, this superb opening from England:

Megarry J. – Errol Flynn was a film actor whose performance gave pleasure to many millions. On June 20, 1909, he was born in Hobart, Tasmania; and on Oct. 14, 1959 he died in Vancou-

> ver, British Columbia. When he was seventeen he was expelled from school in Sydney; and in the next thirty-three years he lived a life [that] was full, lusty, restless and colourful. In his career, in his three marriages, in his friendships, in his quarrels, and in bed with the many women he took there, he lived with zest and irregularity. The lives of film stars are not cast in the ordinary mould; and in some respects Errol Flynn's was more stellar than most. When he died, he posed the only question that I have to decide: Where was he domiciled at the date of his death?

Edward Cox[30] at the beginning of the twentieth century gave good advice to all by encouraging everyone to develop his or her own individual voice:

> There are some authors whose manner is so infectious that it is extremely difficult *not* to catch it. Johnson is one of these. It requires an effort *not* to fall into his formula of speech. But your protection against this danger must be an ever-present conviction that your own style will be the best for you, be it ever so bad or good. You must strive to *be* yourself, to think for yourself, to speak in *your own* manner. What you then say and your *style* of saying it will be in perfect accord and the pleasure of those who read or listen will not be disturbed by a sense of impropriety and unfitness.

We don't recommend imitating Lord Denning but, as a final word on style, we do recommend to you his thoughts on decision writing[31]:

> I hold firmly to the view that – in speeches – or in judgments – if you are to persuade your hearers – or your readers – you must cultivate a style which commands attention. No matter how sound your reasoning, if it is presented in a dull and turgid setting, your hearers – or your readers – will turn aside. They will not stop to listen. They will flick over the pages. But if it is presented in a lively and attractive setting, they will sit up and take notice. They will listen as if spellbound. They will read you with engrossment.

30. COX, Edward W., *The Arts of Writing, Reading and speaking*, Horace Cox, London, 1909.
31. Lord Denning – *The Family Story* (1981; repr. 1982).

CHAPTER VIII

HUMOUR: YES OR NO?

There are very few good judges of humour,
and they don't agree.

Josh Billings

Judicial humour is neither judicial nor humorous. This oft-repeated saying is the point of departure for any discussion of judicial humour in judgments. Unfortunately, in the enthusiasm generated by a perceived opportunity to be clever, some judges forget the pitfalls which go with trying to be funny. Danger lies in offending the parties, the general audience, or both.

Judges must remember the parties believe they have a significant, unresolvable dispute, requiring court intervention. They want justice. They don't want to be the butt of ridicule or to be the target of scorn, sarcasm, or satire. William Prosser, the renowned authority on torts, had no doubts on the subject[32]:

> The bench is not an appropriate place for unseemly levity. The litigant has vital interests at stake. His entire future, or even his life, may be trembling in the balance, and the robed buffoon who makes merry at his expense should be choked with his own wig.

Despite the danger of offending, the Law Reports give too many examples of judges trying to be funny. The extent to which judges in the United States resort to poetry comes as a revelation to Canadian judges. Professor Joyce J. George in her Judicial Opinion Writing Handbook[33], collected numerous examples of

32. William Prosser, *The Judicial Humorist*, 1952.
33. 3rd Ed., William S. Hein & Co., 1993.

poetic licence in American jurisprudence of varying degrees of literary merit. The best of a bad lot is found in Columbus v. Becker34 where neighbours complained, unsuccessfully, of noisy dogs and cats lodged in a veterinary hospital:

> Dogs will howl and cats will yowl
>   When placed in congregation.
> These grating sounds may oft result
>   In human aggravation.
> Laws passed to curb such pesky noise
>   Should fit the situation
> And be so phrased in artful ways
>   To cause no obfuscation.
> In other words, the laws so passed
>   Must plainly be effective.
> Ineptly framed, they lack the force
>   To meet their planned objective.

* * * * *

Judges possibly believe that cases involving animals give more latitude for humour and less cause to give offence. This may be a dubious proposition at best, as any animal rights' activist could confirm. A light touch was achieved by a Newfoundland judge, where an accused was charged with causing unnecessary pain to an animal:

> **Green J.** – When Sammy the cat overturned the kitchen garbage can, little did he know that he was setting in motion a chain of events which would lead to a broken leg, surgery, eight weeks' convalescence in a veterinary hospital and placement in a cat foster home.
>
> The respondent Higgins was charged with wilfully causing unnecessary pain, suffering or injury to an animal contrary to Section 446(1)(a) of the *Criminal Code*. He was acquitted at trial. The prosecutor appeals to this court as a summary conviction appeal court, under Section 813(b) of the *Criminal Code*.

34. (1962) 173 Ohio St. 197.

Background

Mr. Higgins left his downstairs home office to investigate a loud bang in the kitchen. He found the garbage container tipped over and garbage all over the floor. Sammy was arrogantly standing nearby. Believing that Sammy was the culprit, Mr. Higgins decided to teach him a lesson. He took the broom he was using to sweep up the garbage and started to shoo Sammy with it. The startled cat began to run with the respondent in hot pursuit, remonstrating with him all the while. He ran upstairs into the bedroom. Mr. Higgins followed and started rooting at him under the bed with the broom. When Sammy made a break for it at, to use Mr. Higgins words, "very high speed" (also colourfully described by Mr. Higgins as "he went zoop, zoop"), he was pursued down the stairs and into other parts of the house. Essentially, the chase continued throughout the whole house until Sammy ran into the furnace room and stayed there.

* * * * *

Larger animals in Quebec and Alberta prompted these delights:

LeBel J.A. – (translated from the French) Fifteen heifers were peacefully grazing in a meadow near Arthabaska, during the summer of 1983. Impregnated at an untimely moment by a fellow pasturer, an ineffectively castrated bull, they gave birth to calves of dubious lineage. These unfortunate pregnancies lead to an action in damages by their owner ...

Miller J. – It is not very often that a member of the Court of Queen's Bench of Alberta gets an opportunity to hear a civil trial where a Siberian tiger mauls a man. Needless to say, especially as our court has not established a complete record of precedents in this area, I am indebted to both counsel for the able and complete manner in which this trial was presented and for their assistance.

The issues in this case are whether the defendants are subject to strict liability or, in the alternative, were they in any way negligent in the operation of a game farm and if so, whether such negligence was the cause of the injuries suffered by the plaintiff when he was severely mauled by a tiger owned by the defendants and exhibited at the Alberta Game Farm.

In British Columbia, at least one dog had its day:

Hogarth J. – In the early evening hours of the 10th day of April A.D. 1991, one of the good citizens of the defendant, the Township of Langley was lawfully ambling along 204th St. in the balmy spring weather, when, with little warning or prior indication, a dog since described and defined by by-law and otherwise as a "dangerous dog" (a matter which is in some dispute), crossed over from the hither side of the street and nipped the right gluteus maximum of this innocent pedestrian. The unfortunate and unhappy event caused a breaking of the skin and bruising, which no matter where, how, or to whomsoever such might obtain, is a traumatic and painful occurrence worthy of litigious consideration and appropriate recompense. And let it be made abundantly clear, the determination of the villain who perpetrated this anguish has not been determined, such matters having been left to another day and forum, as ours is of different concern.

Alarmed and appropriately disturbed, the victim quite properly complained to the authorities who in the persons of the defendants, Nelson and Green, armed with all the legislative majesty and executive powers granted to them by the Township of Langley "Dog Licensing & Large Animal Control and Impounding Bylaw, 1988 No. 25776" and amendments thereto, attended the residence of the plaintiffs and after some "discussion" which apparently became a bit of a dog fight in itself resulting in the attendance of the police, "Robbie", the treasured Kuypers' family dog, was forcibly and unceremoniously seized from his home over the loud protestations of those present including the plaintiff, Darrin Kuypers, who on his mute pet's behalf protested his innocence.

Such protestations were met at least in part with the announcement of the defendants, Nelson or Green, or one of them, which remarkably remain undenied, that they had the power under the above edict not only to seize Robbie but without any judicial process or intervention, quasi or otherwise, execute him on the spot.

No line-up, photo or otherwise for Robbie, no charge, no dramatic readings of the Canine Charter of Rights and Freedoms, no plea, no trial, no application of the ancient and historic presumption of innocence, no appeal to the majesty of the Court of Appeal; guilt or innocence undetermined, Robbie faced the ignominy of almost immediate oblivion.

Thus, Robbie was taken to the Langley pound which, in the eyes of some, at least Robbie, is a far cry from the warmth, solicitude and understanding of home and hearth and which to him was indeed the equivalent of a canine Gulaag.

The plaintiffs, outraged by the effrontery to Robbie's character, insisted that not only shall every dog have his day, but this dog shall have his day in court and such is re-enforced by the evidence of the plaintiff, Dianne Kuypers, who says on her oath that regardless of whatever evidence the defendants were relying on to prove their case (which in truth appears to be nought but hearsay), Robbie at all times material to the fateful incident was in the basement of the Kuypers' home conducting himself with the essence of canine decorum, sober as a judge, if I dare use the phrase, and further was never known, nor by any stretch of the imagination could be known as a "dangerous dog" as defined in the said enactment or otherwise.

*****

When lawyers or professionals are the subject of a decision, fear of offending may also diminish, particularly when the former's accounts are being taxed. In Ontario, a Taxing Master's gentle sarcasm was widely known and appreciated by those members of the Bar not directly affected:

Master McBride – It has often been argued by solicitors that they should be awarded the costs of the taxation reference even if their bill is reduced substantially but the client, in fact, has paid nothing before the reference. A not very exhaustive examination of this proposition impels one to the conclusion that it is sheer nonsense. By way of illustration, suppose a solicitor delivers his bill to his client and included in it is a fee of $1,500. The client, under the shackling influence of a more modest view of the solicitor's worth than that entertained by the solicitor himself, does the only thing he can think to do in the circumstances, he simply does not pay the bill.

Master McBride – It seems to me to be beyond controversy that a minimum tariff is not designed to benefit clients as a class or the public generally. These tariffs are formulated by the members of the bar in each county, or their representatives. One need not drink very deeply at the well of cynicism to entertain at least a fleeting suspicion that those who have formulated these tariffs and have been responsible for their amendment from time to time may perhaps have been at least marginally motivated by a barely discernible degree of professional self-interest, usually less euphemistically referred to as **greed**, among the working classes.

* * * * *

In Australia, a judge used a nautical metaphor to wonderful effect:

Heerey J. – I am satisfied that the advice of a competent accountant in the present case would have been sufficiently clear, given the manifest risks and dangers of the scheme and its unsuitability for these clients, to have deterred the applicants from investing. Perhaps more importantly, a competent accountant, upon an examination of the scheme, would not have introduced his clients to Gray & Winter in the first place. Like Ulysses' oarsmen, their ears would have been blocked to keep out the siren song of Gray & Winter. [...]

The Coles Myer building investment scheme was like an overloaded and unseaworthy ship setting out on a long voyage. Given exceptionally fair winds and calm seas she might conceivably have reached her destination. However she was always to be at severe risk from ordinary perils of the seas. The fact that what sunk her was a cyclone of 50-year severity hardly absolves those who caused her to put to sea.

* * * * *

Criminal cases lend themselves to the mock-heroic style:

Tyndale J.A. – It was a dark and stormy night in the old Capital on that Saturday in March of 1983. Few people were abroad in the streets in the cold wind and driving rain. A little shop on the corner of Chemin Ste-Foy and Avenue Marguerite Bourgeois was a cosy oasis of light and warmth. In the shop were two little old ladies; one was Mme Jeannine Blouin-Côté, the proprietress, and the other was her younger sister, Mlle Madeleine Blouin, behind the counter at the cash. Business was slow, and the ladies were thinking of closing early when suddenly, a little before 9 by the Molson clock on the wall, the door opened to admit a gust of wind, a shower of rain, and a man.

The newcomer was clad in a ski-jacket glistening with rain drops, brown suede shoes, and a stocking mask. He pointed a gloved hand like a pistol at Mlle Blouin, and with threats of violence uttered in language shocking to the ladies demanded all the money in the shop. Mlle Blouin was terrified, but she managed to scrabble out all the paper money in the till, and to throw it at the robber's feet. As he stooped to retrieve it, Mme Côté came up and began to kick him, but he managed to stuff the money in his jacket and gain the street. Mme Côté, nothing daunted, gave chase, shouting "*Stop thief!*" and caught up to the fugitive in front of Camille's Restaurant. "*Will you leave me alone*", he cried, and dropping two $5 bills in front of her made his escape in the direction of the Holland Building, not running, but walking fast with a curious loping stride. [...]

* * * * *

Unsurprisingly, encounters between the sexes have not escaped judicial notice. The following classic British understatement appeared in the early 70's:

Edmund Davies LJ – This is about as extraordinary a case as my brethren and I have ever heard either on the Bench or while at the Bar. Stephen William George Collins was convicted on 29th October 1971 at Essex Assizes of burglary with intent to commit rape and he was sentenced to 21 months' imprisonment. He is a 19 year old youth, and he appeals against that conviction by the certificate of the trial judge. The terms in which that certificate is expressed reveal that the judge was clearly troubled about the case and the conviction.

Let me relate the facts. Were they put into a novel or portrayed on the stage, they would be regarded as being so improbable as to be unworthy of serious consideration and as verging at times on farce. At about two o'clock in the early morning of Saturday, 24th July 1971, a young lady of 18 went to bed at her mother's home in Colchester. She had spent the evening with her boyfriend. She had taken a certain amount of drink, and it may be that this fact affords some explanation of her inability to answer satisfactorily certain crucial questions put to her. She has the habit of sleeping without wearing night apparel in a bed which is very near the lattice-type window of her room. At one stage on her evidence she seemed to be saying that the bed was close up against the window which, in accordance with her practice, was wide open. In the photographs which we have before us, however, there appears to be a gap of some sort between the two, but the bed was clearly quite near the window. At about 3.30 or 4.00 a m she awoke and she then saw in the moonlight a vague form crouched in the open window. She was unable to remember, and this is important, whether the form was on the outside of the window sill or on that part of the sill which was inside the room, and for reasons which will later become clear, that seemingly narrow point is of crucial importance. The young lady then realised several things: first of all that the form in the window was that of a male; secondly that he was a naked male; and thirdly that he was a naked male with an erect penis. She also saw in the moonlight that his hair was blond. She thereupon leapt to the conclusion that her boyfriend, with whom for some time she had been on terms of regular and frequent sexual intimacy, was paying her an ardent nocturnal visit. She promptly sat up in bed, and the man descended from the sill and joined her in bed and they had full sexual intercourse. But there was something about him which made her think that things were not as they usually were between her and her boyfriend. The length of his hair, his voice as they exchanged what was described as `love talk', and other features led her to the conclusion that somehow there was something different. So she turned on the bed-side light, saw that her companion was not her boyfriend and slapped the face of the intruder, who was none other than the appellant. He said to her, `Give me a good time tonight`, and got hold of her arm, but she bit him and told him to go. She then went into the bathroom and he promptly vanished.

The complainant said that she would not have agreed to intercourse if she had known that the person entering her room was not her boyfriend. But there was no suggestion of any force having been used on her, and the intercourse which took place was undoubtedly effected with no resistance on her part.

The appellant was seen by the police at about 10.30 a m later that same morning. According to the police, the conversation which took place then elicited these points: He was very lustful the previous night. He had taken a lot of drink, and we may here note that drink (which to him is a very real problem) had brought this young man into trouble several times before, but never for an offence of this kind. He went on to say that he knew the complainant because he had worked around her house. On this occasion, desiring sexual intercourse – and according to the police evidence he had added that he was determined to have a girl, by force if necessary, although that part of the police evidence he challenged – he went on to say that he walked around the house, saw a light in an upstairs bedroom, and he knew that this was the girl's bedroom. What he could see inside through the wide open window was a girl who was naked and asleep. So he descended the ladder and stripped off all his clothes, with the exception of his socks, because apparently he took the view that if the girl's mother entered the bedroom it would be easier to effect a rapid escape if he had his socks on than if he was in his bare feet. That is a matter about which we are not called on to express any view, and would in any event find ourselves unable to express one. Having undressed, he then climbed the ladder and pulled himself up on to the window sill. His version of the matter is that he was pulling himself in when she awoke. She then got up and knelt on the bed, she put her arms around his neck and body, and she seemed to pull him into the bed.

* * * * *

A marriage of convenience to obtain landed immigrant status in Canada prompted an Ontario judge to philosophize on the institution of marriage:

> **Chartrand J.** – The lady petitioner, a Canadian resident, went to Kenya to marry a citizen of that country. After the ceremony, the parties immediately parted. The petitioner stayed at the home of friends and slept there alone for several days. Then she took the aeroplane back to Canada without seeing her alleged husband again. Indeed, I do not have even the evidence of a kiss between the parties.
>
> As soon as a year elapsed since the said ceremony, the lady launched this petition for divorce on the ground of non-consummation for over a year.
>
> I have no evidence on her part that she was willing, ready and able to have sexual relations with the respondent; indeed, the conduct of the parties in Kenya immediately after the form of marriage points to a pre-nuptial agreement between the parties to abstain, *inter alia,* from sexual relations. So she cannot be heard now to complain about non-consummation when she got exactly what she bargained for.[...]
>
> Romance, as a spur to marriage, is a rather modern phenomenon, and limited at that; passionate love is not an essential element of the marriage status, though a welcome one.
>
> A marriage is not vitiated because a party is motivated into embracing this status by considerations extraneous to love; indeed, most marriages are entered into with a certain degree of practical reasons, and sometimes those reasons are predominant ones: for example, one does marry to please his parents or to avoid conscription in the army. This state of affairs may appear mean and unrapturing to a romantic soul, but then life is not a novel.

* * * * *

There is no shortage of unintentional humour in the Law Reports. In the late 30s four out of five judges in the Ontario Court of Appeal permitted accused's counsel to argue for an acquittal, although the relief sought was a new trial. The fifth judge was flabbergasted at the effrontery of the accused's counsel and the lack of wisdom of his four colleagues:

> Mr. Hope appeared dazed at the assurance of counsel for the accused and seemed not to know what he ought to do or say. I did not long await his decision but protested immediately against such a radical change in the appeal. To my amazement, opinions directly opposed to mine were at once expressed by three if not four, if four then all, of my associates. Nevertheless, I renewed my protest, but when the same opposition continued to be manifested, I subsided with the best grace I could assume. I confess I entertained momentarily the thought of leaving the Bench, but almost as suddenly realizing the consequences that such action would entail, abandoned the idea. Mr. Greer then continued with his new appeal and proceeded with what seemed to me, owing to the several hours' study which I had previously given to the case, a one-sided, inaccurate and only partial review of the evidence, with citations of such law as he thought properly applied. During his presentation, I could not but observe that he often took occasion to consult Mr. Maloney. If the learned and competent senior counsel was without information that he thus appeared to procure from his junior, I thought it not improbable that the members of the Court might misinform themselves on matters regarded with doubt by Mr. Greer as, with all respect, I think they did. I was quite willing to agree that each member of the Court had the same right to form his opinion as I had to form mine. However, I doubted that anyone of them had devoted as much time as I had to the consideration of the evidence and exhibits, especially on the evening that intervened during Mr. Greer's argument. I had also, I thought, some little advantage owing to my long and intimate connection with the County of Renfrew. This began in my teen age with rod and gun along the Ottawa; then, with rod only, as far West as the Little Opeongo; then acting at Pembroke in my private practice and in the capacity of counsel for the Crown, during more than five years, visiting annually every section of the vast riding of South Renfrew; and, finally, until about sixteen years ago, when appointed to this Court, presiding at several sittings of assize, etc., held

at Pembroke. I think I thus acquired a much greater knowledge than any of my associates in the Court of the county and its generally industrious, frugal, peaceful, moral and law-abiding inhabitants. As I usually pass the long vacation at my cottage on a paved highway up the Ottawa, I have taken advantage in recent years of that facility to motor quite often to the Town of Renfrew and to points along and off the Opeongo Road as distant as Burdenell and Combermere. I have thus renewed old memories of this road as it leads southerly through farms owned by members of a pioneer family of high standing, the Carswells, Allan Carswell's south of the road, on its left, as one goes from the business and residential parts of the town, and James Carswell's on the right along the same course. While I merely think it probable that I can better visualize the terrain than persons who have never seen it, and better understand the evidence where it is indefinite, I am quite certain that neither I nor any member of the Court can have the same knowledge of it as had the members of the jury after the plan and several of the photographs had been explained before their eyes and they had actually, as stated, visited and, no doubt examined, the localities referred to by witnesses whose testimony the jury had, previous to their visit to the Town of Renfrew, found difficulty in understanding. But apart from the advantages, if any, of my personal recollections, I felt more and more firmly convinced at the close of Mr. Greer's presentation of the appeal, that it would be improper for the Court to substitute its necessarily limited acquaintance with the facts for the careful and long deliberated verdict of a jury better qualified than any appellate Court to render judgment on the matters in dispute. I still adhere strongly to that opinion.

* * * * *

Contrast the above with this witty description of local practice in Scotland:

Lord Devlin – My Lords, when a person in the Isle of Islay wishes to send goods to the mainland he goes into the office of MacBrayne (the respondents) in Port Askaig which is conveniently combined with the local post office. There he is presented with a document headed "conditions" containing three of four thousand words of small print divided into 27 paragraphs. Beneath them there is a space for the sender's signature which he puts below his statement in quite legible print that he thereby agrees to ship on the conditions stated above. The appellant, Mr. McCutcheon, described the negotiations which preceded the making of this formidable contract in the following terms: "Q. Tell us about that document; how did you come to sign it? "A. You just walk in the office and the document is filled up "ready and all you have to do is to sign your name and go out. "Q. Did you ever read the conditions? A. No. Q. Did you know "what was in them? A. No."

There are many other passages in which Mr. McCutcheon and his brother-in-law, Mr. McSporran, endeavour more or less successfully to appease the forensic astonishment aroused by this statement. People shipping calves, Mr. McCutcheon said (he was dealing with an occasion when he had shipped 36 calves), had not much time to give to the reading. Asked to deal with another occasion when he was unhampered by livestock, he said that people generally just tried to be in time for the boat's sailing; it would, he thought, take half a day to read and understand the conditions and then he would miss the boat. In another part of his evidence he went so far as to say that if everybody took time to read the document, "MacBrayne's office "would be packed out the door." Mr. McSporran evidently thought the whole matter rather academic because, as he pointed out, there was no other way to send a car.

* * * * *

For a capsule comment on *stare decisis* in Alberta:

Master Funduk – Any legal system which has a judicial appeals process, inherently creates a pecking order for the judiciary regarding where judicial decisions stand on the legal ladder.

I am bound by decisions of Queen's Bench Judges, by decisions of the Alberta Court of Appeal and by decisions of the Supreme Court of Canada. Very simply, Masters in Chambers of a superior trial Court occupy the bottom rung of the superior Courts' judicial ladder.

I do not overrule decisions of a judge of this Court. The judicial pecking order does not permit little peckers to overrule big peckers. It is the other way around.

* * * * *

In the last century, the enthusiastic expenses of a municipal council cause the Chief Justice to reveal himself as more than an amateur oenophile[35]:

Sir P. O'Brien C.J. – I now come to deal with the expenditure in respect of the lunch. Now I think it is relevant to refer to the character of this luncheon. I have before me the items in the bill. Amongst the list of wines are two dozen champagne, Ayala, 1885 – a very good brand – at 84s. a dozen; one dozen Marcobrunn hock – a very nice hock; one dozen Château Margaux – an excellent claret; one dozen fine old Dublin whiskey – the best whiskey that can be got; one case of Ayala; six bottles of Amontillado sherry – a stimulating sherry; and the ninth item is some more fine Dublin whiskey! Then Mr. Lovell supplies the "*dinner*" (this was a dinner, not a mere luncheon!) including all attendance, at 10s. per head. There is an allowance for brakes; one box of cigars, 100; coachmen's dinner; beer, stout, minerals in syphons, and ice for wine. There is dessert, and there are sandwiches, and an allowance for four glasses broken – a very small number broken under the circumstances.

In sober earnestness, what was this luncheon and outing? It seems to me to have been a picnic on an expensive scale. What authority is there for it? No statutable authority exists. By what principle of our common law is it sustainable? By none that I can see. In *M'Evoy's Case* (1), to which I have already referred, there was a question of maintaining the Mansion House, being the property of the Corporation. But this is a question of providing a sumptuous repast for the members of the Corporation on the Wicklow hills. It is not certainly for the benefit of the property of the Corporation, or of the rate-paying citizens of Dublin, that the members of the Corporation should lunch sumptuously. I asked for statute of for case, but neither was cited. The

35. *The Queen* v. *Drury*, [1894] The Irish Reports, vol. II, 495.

Solicitor-General in his most able argument – I have always to guard myself against his plausibility – appealed pathetically to common sense; he asked, really with tears in his voice, whether the members of the Corporation should starve; he drew a most gruesome picture; he represented that the members of the Corporation would really traverse the Wicklow hills in a spectral condition, unless they were sustained by lunch. I do not know, whether he went so far as Ayala, Marcobrunn, Château Margaux, old Dublin whiskey and cigars. In answer to the pathetic appeal of the Solicitor-General, we do not say that the members of the Corporation are not to lunch. But we do say that they are not to do so at the expense of the citizens of Dublin. They cannot banquet at their expense in the Mansion House, and, in our opinion, they cannot lunch at their expense in Wicklow.

*****

In the above extracts, some judges have succeeded in adding a dash of humour without wounding anybody in doing so. Others may have failed. It is for you to decide. Be careful. Better to avoid the attempt entirely rather than be guilty of bad taste or offending anyone involved in the proceedings.

CONCLUSION

To pronounce a judgment or to write one is difficult. To write one well is more difficult. To take the necessary time requires determination and steadfastness.

Whether scratching with a pen or staring at a screen, only writers know the solitary joy of overcoming a difficulty in drafting.

To help overcome difficulties in drafting, here is a summary of the suggestions in this handbook:

1) make an outline of the decision and follow it;

2) write simply;

3) use language that others can understand [including the wider audience];

4) catch your reader's interest with an interesting beginning that summarizes the events which lead to the dispute;

5) announce the issues early;

6) reason rigorously;

7) be concise; be considerate;

8) and revise.

In closing, let us offer some encouragement for the adoption of the principles of good decision writing we have tried to outline. We believe their adoption can lead to being right in law more often than otherwise. No demonstrable proof exists for this belief except an analogy from human experience. We are all familiar with seeking a colleague's help in answering a question. In explaining the question so the colleague can understand, we arrive at the answer ourselves. So it is with decision writing – the rigorous application of sound principles will lead the way to the right conclusion.

APPENDIX I

To require a writer to abandon the words in the left column would be silly. Nevertheless, their overuse makes weighty prose. For a change in diet, consider the low-fat substitutes in the right column.

Instead of:	**Consider:**
A	
abbreviate	shorten
accelerate	speed up
accompany	go with
accomplish	carry out, do
accordingly	so
accumulate	gather
accurate	correct, exact, right
achieve	do, make
acquaint with	tell
acquire	gain, get
additional	more, add, other
adequate	enough
adjacent	next to

advance planning	planning
advantageous	helpful
advert	refer, mention
aircraft	plane
alteration	change
ameliorate	improve
anticipate	expect
a number of	some, approximately, about
apparent	clear, plain
apprise	inform
as a means of	to
ascertain	find out
ask a question	ask
assistance	help
at the present time	now

B

be responsible for	handle
by means of	by, with

C

category	class, group

combined	joint
commence	start
comply with	follow
comprise	form, include, make up
concerning	about, on
conclude	close, end
concur	agree
consequently	so
constitutes	is, forms, makes up
construct	build
contains	has
continue	keep on
contribute	give
currently	now

D

delete	cut, drop
deleterious	harmful
demonstrate	show
depart	leave
designate	appoint, choose
desire	wish

desist	stop
disburse	pay, pay out
disclose	show
discontinue	drop, stop
disseminate	issue, mail, send out
due to the fact that	since
during the time that	while

E

echelons	level
effect	make
elect	choose, pick
eliminate	cut, drop
elucidate	explain
encounter	meet
endeavour	try
ensure	make sure
establish	set up, prove
evaluate	check, rate
evident	clear
evince	show, display
examine	look at

expedite	hasten
expertise	skill
explain	show, tell
F	
facilitate	help
factor	cause, reason
failed to	didn't
feasible	can be done, workable
females	women
final	last
finalize	complete, finish
for a period of	for
for example	such as
forfeit	give up, lose
for the purpose of	because
forward	send
function	role, work
H	
however	but
I	
identical	same

immediately	at once, now
implement	carry out, do
in accordance with	by, following, under
in addition	also, besides, too
in an effort to	to
in as much as	since
in a timely manner	on time, promptly
in conjunction with	with
incorporate	blend, join, merge
indicate	show, wtire down
indication	sign
initial	first
initiate	start
in lieu of	instead of
in order that	so
in order to	to
in regard to	about, concerning
in the course of	during, in
in the event that	if, when
it is essential	must

J

join together	join

L

legislation	law
limited number	few
locate	find
location	place, scene, site

M

magnitude	size
maintain	keep, support
majority	greatest, longest, most
males	men
minimize	decrease, reduce
modify	change
most of the time	usually

N

necessitate	cause
no later than	by
notify	let know, tell
numerous	many, most

O

objective	aim, goal
observe	see
obtain	get
optimum	best
option	choice

P

parameters	limits
participate	take part
perform	do
permit	let
personnel	people, staff
pertaining	about, on
point in time	now, when
portion	part
position	place, put
possess	have, own
prepared	ready
previous	earlier, past
previously	before
prior to	before

procedures	ways, rules
proceed	do, go on, try
proficiency	skill
proposes to	means to, suggests
provide	give, supply
provided that	if
purchase	buy
R	
reason for	why
recapitulate	sum up
reduce	cut
reflect	say, show
regarding	about, of, on
relating to	about, on
relocation	move
remain	stay
remainder	rest
render	give, make
request	ask
require	must, need
requirement	need

reside	live
retain	keep
review	check, go over
S	
similar to	like
solicit	ask for
state	say
state-of-the-art	latest
submit	give, send
subsequent	later, next
subsequently	after, then
substantial	large, real, strong
sufficient	enough
T	
terminate	end, stop
therefore	so
therein	there
timely	prompt
time period	time, period
U	
utilize	use

V

value	cost, worth
viable	practical, workable

W

whenever	when
whereas	since
with reference to	about
with the exception of	except for

APPENDIX II

	Transitions		Purpose
1	and or, nor also moreover	furthermore indeed in fact first, second...	To add something.
2	for instance for example for one thing	similarly likewise	To illustrate or expand a point.
3	therefore thus so and so hence consequently	finally on the whole all in all in other words in short	To summarize.
4	frequently occasionally in particular in general	specifically especially usually	To add a qualifying illustration.
5	of course no doubt doubtless	to be sure granted (that) certainly	To recognize a different point of view.
6	but however yet on the contrary	not at all surely no	To reverse a train of thought.

7	still nevertheless notwithstanding		To return to the main point, after a concession.
8	although though whereas		To attach a concession to the main point.
9	because since for		To connect a reason to a statement.
10	if provided in case	unless lest when	To qualify and restrict a general idea.
11	as if as though even if		To consider a hypothetical condition that supports a point.

SELECTIVE BIBLIOGRAPHY

ALDISERT, Rugero J., *Opinion Writing*, West Publishing, St. Paul, Minnesota, 1990.

BURNHAM, Sophy, *For writers only*, Random House Canada, 1994.

Canadian Guide to Uniform Legal Citation, 1992 Trustees of the McGill Law Journal Trust Fund, 3rd Edition, Carswell.

CONSTANZO, Margot, *Legal Writing – (Essential Legal Skills Series)*, Series Editor Julie MacFarlane, 1993, Cavendish Publishing Limited, London.

COX, Edward W., *The Arts of Writing, Reading and speaking*, Horace Cox, London, 1909.

DICK, Robert C., *Legal Drafting*, Carswell Co. Ltd., 3rd Ed., 1995.

DOYLE, Margaret, *The A-Z of Non-Sexist Language*, The Women's Press, London, 1995.

ÉTIEMBLE and Jeannine ÉTIEMBLE, *L'art d'écrire*, Éd. Seghers, Paris, 1970.

GEORGE, Joyce J., *Judicial Opinion Writing Handbook*, third edition, William S. Hein & Co. Buffalo, 1993.

KOLB, Harold H. Jr., *A Writer's Guide: The essential points*, Harcourt Brace Jovanovich Inc., 1980.

KOMAR, Roman N., *Reasons for judgment: A handbook for judges and other judicial officers*, Butterworths, 1980.

KRAMER, Melinda G., LEGGETT, Glenn, MEAD, C. David, *Prentice-Hall Handbook for Writers*, Prentice-Hall Inc., N.Y. 1995.

LEFLAR, Robert A., *Appellate Judicial Opinions Chap. 7 – The Writing of Opinions*, The Institute of Judicial Administration, New York University, West Publishing Co., St. Paul, Minnesota, 1974.

LEFLAR, Robert A., *International Operating Procedures of Appellate Courts – Chap. 3: The Decisional Process*, American Bar Foundation, Chicago, 1976.

MacMILLAN, Lord, *The Writing of Judgments*, (1948) 26 C.B.R. 491.

MAGGIO, Rosalie, *The Non-Sexist Wordfinder: A Dictionary of Gender-free Usage*, Beacon Press, Boston, 1989.

MILLER, Casey and SWIFT, Kate, *The Handbook of Non-Sexist Writing*, The Women's Press, 2nd British Edition, London, 1989.

RAIMES, Ann, *Keys for Writers*, A brief handbook, Hunter College, New York, 1996.

RAYMOND, James C., *Writing (Is an Unnatural Act)*, Harper & Row, New York, 1980.

RAYMOND, James C. and GOLDFARB, Ronald L., *Clear Understandings: A guide to legal writing*, Random House Inc., 1982.

SEIDL, J. and McMORDIE, W., *English Idioms and how to use them*, Oxford university Press, fifth edition, 1988.

SMITH, George Rose, *A Primer of Opinion Writing, For Four New Judges*, 21 Ark. L.R. 197.

STRUNK, William Jr. and WHITE, E.B., *The Elements of Style*, third edition, Collier & MacMillan Canada Ltd., 1979.

TURABIAN, Kate L., *A Manual for Writers*, fourth edition, The University of Chicago Press, 1973.

WINTERS, Glenn R., *Handbook for Judges: An anthology of inspirational and educational writings for members of the judiciary – A primer of opinion writing for four new judges – George Rose Smith,* (p. 123), The American Judicature Society, 1975.

WITKIN, B.E., *Manual on Appellate Court Opinions – Chap. IV: Mechanics of Drafting Opinions; Chap. VII: Style,* The California Center for Judicial Education and Research, Berkely, West Publishing Co., St. Paul, Minnesota, 1977.

YOGIS & CHRISTIE, *Legal Writing and Research Manual,* 4th edition, Butterworths, 1994.

ANALYTICAL INDEX

-Q-

-R-

-S-

-T-

-U-

-V-

-W-